GROUNDED

A Journey Beneath The Surface

Ann Kronlage

1st WORLD
PUBLISHING

GROUNDED

A Journey Beneath The Surface

Ann Kronlage

© Ann Kronlage 2008

Published by 1stWorld Publishing
P.O. Box 2211 Fairfield, Iowa 52556
tel: 641-209-5000 • fax: 641-209-3001
web: www.1stworldpublishing.com

First Edition

LCCN: 2008935227
SoftCover ISBN: 978-1-4218-9013-5
HardCover ISBN: 978-1-4218-9012-8
eBook ISBN: 978-1-4218-9014-2

Breathtaking

"Panic is your greatest enemy." He said to me as we prepared for descent into the Caribbean Sea. I believed him since he was the dive master and I the clueless beginner. I listened to Fernando explain the basics of diving after he agreed to take my fifty dollars US in exchange for escorting me on a dive off the coast of Puerto Morales, Mexico. My older sister Marie and her husband Bill had encouraged me to go on this trip with them to this beautifully isolated part of the Yucatan. They were educated and experienced in scuba diving and hauled their gear all the way from California to Cancun, where I met them at the airport. I flew in from St. Louis with a small suitcase and an eagerness to have the first real vacation since having babies in four years.

I never went under the water like a real scuba diver except for a resort dive on my honeymoon in the Bahamas with Chase who was ready to try anything. At 24, I thought Chase was fearless. Now 28, I knew better and had decided to practice a little fearlessness of my own.

With gear for four people we barely had room for ourselves on the small boat with a motor hanging off the back that Fernando pulled like a lawnmower to get started. Fernando calmly drove the boat through the awakening sea. The coastline, littered with dried kelp, patiently waited as the sun climbed across the clear blue sky. Marie and Bill looked unworried. They seemed to understand about panic being the enemy.

Fernando stopped the boat, stood up and began assembling

his gear and mine for the dive. He had done this a million times, didn't seem at all concerned about someone like me, with no experience or training, diving in with him. I quietly introduced myself to the panic that was rising in me. I had gone through fear before in my past, big fear, the kind of fear that everyone asked "How did you do it?" about. I had words of wisdom for people when they asked. How I just went through my fear. I talked big for someone who was once again being humbled. I couldn't back out now but God what was I doing?

Marie and Bill and Fernando agreed on a time that we would all return to the boat. Marie and Bill descended. Now it was my turn. A mask was strapped on my head with a snorkel attached. A regulator rested in my mouth and delivered compressed air from the tank velcroed on the back of my vest which inflated or deflated according to a button that Fernando pushed. A weight belt to offset any buoyancy my body might experience once underwater was tightly buckled to my waist. A fin fit on my right foot only since my left foot was a prosthesis and from experience the day before, snorkeling, I decided better left on the boat. Underneath all that I wore a bathing suit and long t-shirt. Fernando fit his gear on himself, helped me with mine then told me it was time to get in the water.

Babies do this in reverse every time they are born, I thought to myself as I went from easy, comfortable air to the powerful force of salty sea water encasing me in its gentleness yet reminding me I could die if I wasn't careful. The air from the tank had to be coaxed from my mouthpiece by deliberate inhalations.

I held onto Fernando's hand as I watched him. He seemed so comfortable with all of this. His vivid blue eyes met mine and he signaled okay? with his hands and nodding head. I answered with an okay sign on my right hand. We went down about ten feet below the surface when my arm swung across my face and knocked the regulator out of my mouth. Fernando saw this and turned again to face me, looking into my eyes. I looked at him for what to do but there was nothing but a calm observing gaze staring back at me. I grabbed the regulator that had drifted on its tube to my right side, placed it in my mouth as before and blew all the air inside of me out. Bubbles exploded out and I knew it was safe to take a breath. I did and Fernando asked me again okay? with his hand. I signaled okay and we proceeded to a deeper destination. I felt like a newborn baby as I allowed myself to be led by Fernando and slowly we moved through the water for about a half hour.

How did that happen? How did I get through that without dying? Without giving in to panic? I didn't know the answer. I didn't know the answer eleven years earlier when I encountered panic beyond my imagination.

Eleven years earlier

I had plenty of reasons to steal my father's car.

If you followed my father around the house, besides dying of boredom, you'd ask yourself, "Is that all he cares about—cigarettes, catatonic children and television?"

I knew better. I knew he loved his car.

He declared himself a Chevy man but for one—a 1971 BMW 316i. Both German, he and the car even looked alike— short, squarish and milky yellow colored. If he never shared anything with me, he did teach me to drive that car. He taught me to maneuver the five layers of transmission the way he wished he could maneuver through life.

First gear felt like intimacy. Some people needed it, but you had to be sensitive to its subtlety to appreciate it. My father liked the fact that in a BMW he could get away with ignoring it entirely. Without a stutter, that amazing car could take off from a dead stop, in second gear. Second gear played the role of education for my father. With a degree, you could get ahead in the world and distance yourself from that nonsense called emotions his wife always tried to talk to him about. He resigned himself to its necessity so he could stay on the good side of a God the Catholic Church and his heritage told him to fear. Faith stood in his mind as a necessity that didn't require too much time, as it was with third gear. Soon we shifted into fourth. Fourth seemed like respect. Acknowledgement by others, whether it took the form of fear, obedience or acquiescence, was my father's idea of respect. Respect, in his mind, was a given after one lived long enough, went to school long enough or sired enough children. When you were given respect, you knew real power, my father said with fifth gear. Like fifth gear and his idea of power, all actions toward it were done solely for the purpose of getting to it. Fifth gear promised unlimited speed, unlimited freedom and unlimited possibilities. Fifth gear was the solitary man on the mountain who believed that he alone had made it to the top.

When you saw my mother you'd ask, "Why does she always act either too busy or too exhausted?"

"Hang around the good-looking girls and you'll be more likely to find a boyfriend." my mother advised me. So I hung out with Rebecca, one of the most unlikely candidates for my mother's idea of good-looking. Rebecca had a mean, hilarious sense of humor. Her mother died of cancer when she was ten and her father remarried a woman Rebecca grew to hate. We had plenty of reasons to be best friends.

In sophomore year of high school, Rebecca and I went on a split shift schedule. 8000 kids in one school finally got the administration to figure out that they needed to break the numbers into three high schools. Problem was there stood just one building. The year they finally started construction on East High and West High, we all packed into Central High's building on split shifts. Rebecca and I rode the same bus that picked us up at 6AM. The good news was at 1:00 in the afternoon when we got home, the nine other people in my family were

Ann Kronlage

gone and my parents' station wagon in the driveway beckoned us to take it for a ride. Both of us had taken driver's ed in freshmen year. Nothing could stop us from giving in to the temptation of grand theft auto.

That first afternoon Rebecca and I felt like a couple of wild women 'til we got to the gas station. In 1975, when you pulled your car up to a gas pump, attendants—men usually—came up to the driver's window and asked "What'll it be?"

"Two gallons." I said, trying to sound experienced. The guy gave me a confused look but pumped exactly two gallons into the tank.

That afternoon of scanning fast food parking lots, where drive-thrus didn't exist yet and only old people or mothers and their young children hung out, convinced us to switch to late-night cruises.

My father was so predictable you could set your clock by his boring routine. Right after Johnny Carson, he turns off the TV, walks to the bathroom, takes a piss with the door open, then collapses onto his side of the bed, across from my sleeping mother, with his clothes still on. After about ten minutes, I go upstairs from my basement bedroom and pretend to need something from the kitchen. Their bedroom is right off the kitchen so I can hear if he is snoring or not. His loud pig snorts tell me he is deep asleep.

Stealing the keys off my father's dresser, ten feet from his snoring nose, was so easy, I sometimes wished he would catch me in the act. The thought of his surprised, angry reaction when he found out painted a big smile across my face.

"Marie's car's still gone. You sure she won't notice the car gone when she gets back?" Rebecca asked me out on the drive-way.

"Screw it." I said. "She'll be too tired this late at night to notice." Rebecca laughed at the idea and we climbed into my father's pride and joy.

I pushed my left foot down on the clutch and grabbed hold of the locked steering wheel. The car rolled backwards down the slope of the driveway. Once the back wheels touched the curb, I yanked my foot off the clutch and the engine started itself.

Rebecca's good to have along as shotgun. She's ready to go anywhere and do anything. Like the time she chose her old boyfriend Jon's doorbell to ring. At 1AM, Jon's mother opened the door in robe and slippers and carrying what looked like a long barreled shotgun, chasing Rebecca to the end of the driveway. I watched from the driver's seat across the street, ready to peel out as soon as Rebecca made it to the car. With the headlights off, we got away, not laughing till we were several blocks down the street.

That night we got back about 3AM. No one was waiting up for us. Marie's car was in the driveway. It looked like we were in the clear. By 10AM, I woke up to Marie saying, "Dad knows you took the car. I woke him up last night after I got home and didn't see it in the driveway. You're in trouble now." My sister was such a rag who never failed to turn her back on me.

I was scared but excited to see the old man pissed to the max, and curious about what he might do. It was actually disappointing when all he said was, "Don't ever do that again." I couldn't believe it! He didn't raise his voice or his hand to me. "Don't ever take Rebecca with you again." He said, just to have the last word. You could always keep him satisfied if you let him have the last word. I agreed that I wouldn't do it again or take Rebecca with me, even though I thought NOT IN A MILLION YEARS would I leave my partner in crime at home.

The way my dad reacted, so calmly, after finding out I stole his car, made me feel like he threw cold water all over me. I didn't feel like fighting him anymore, just like getting out of the house as much as possible, away from my family.

Ann Kronlage

When I wanted to, I knew how to play the good girl. At least that's the way the teachers and principals treated me, like because I was a cheerleader and had near perfect grades, I was some kind of could-do-no-wrong. The opposite was true at home. The last time I showed my mother my straight A report card her only comment was, "Anybody could get straight A's from a public high school." GOD I was dying to get away from them all.

Staying out of the house was easy with cheerleading from early summer till late spring, gymnastics team in the fall, babysitting on any available evening and track team in the spring.

I never really had friends who were cheerleaders but I loved being a cheerleader. When I was little, I sat in front of the television and dreamed of being one of the June Taylor dancers on the Carol Burnett show. Cheerleading was all about dancing for me. I could see kids in the stands at the football games or basketball games laughing at all the cheerleaders, waiting for one of us to make the next mistake, but I felt so good I didn't care. Every inch of my body tingled. I was in love with the feeling of moving.

"You're too big for gymnastics." The coach told me. Funny, she was about my size—five feet eight inches tall and 150 pounds. She coached what she admitted to me she could never do. She and I both knew, though, that the gymnastics team never cut anybody, so she would never get rid of me. It didn't matter that she never put me in competition and that she insulted my body. I was in love with the feeling of moving like a dancer. I loved the two hour practices after school every day, when the coach ignored me because I wasn't competition material. I could do whatever I wanted. I loved feeling my body get stronger and even the coach had to admit that I could move gracefully.

Track was another of those teams that never cut anybody.

Once again, I never really competed but I loved the movement and the chance to watch the boys' track team that practiced the same time we did.

"Moose" is what some guy in my neighborhood who's a year behind me at school yelled when I walked past him one day. Thanks asshole, I love you too, I wanted to say when I thought about it later. I always think of the good lines after it's too late. I tell myself I will never trust that guy or do any favors for him, like the problem's taken care of. But buried in the back of the closet is the sad little me feeling very hurt and wanting to magically transform from frog into beautiful princess and make him sorry for the rest of his life he ever said that to me.

My idea of magically transforming one day was to not eat for as long as possible and hope I could lose some weight. I couldn't even last a day before I got dizzy, tired and too hungry to do anything but think about food. So much for my shot at being a beautiful princess.

My mother always looked at me with disappointment in her eyes. I could never be her ideal—Cindy Stafford (a girl from our church)—thin, long legs with good skin, teeth and hair. I had some of it, the good hair, teeth and skin, but my muscular, short legs would never be worthy of anyone's praise, especially my mother's. She always made fun of her own short, "fat" legs in front of her bedroom closet mirror, with my father standing by, cheering her on.

Which brings me to one of the reasons I babysat—to get away from my parents when gymnastics, track and cheerleading couldn't get me out of the house. Also I love kids, most kids anyway. There have been a few total brats, like Johnny what's his name who locked himself in the closet, screaming that he wasn't going anywhere, after his mother left me with instructions to take his brother, sister and him to the neighborhood pool to swim. I sat down in the most comfortable chair in their living room, told the confused brother and sister we weren't going anywhere till Johnny came out and enjoyed reading Mom's magazines and watching TV with the disappointed siblings. He stayed in there the whole time and I knew I would never be asked to accept another job for that family again.

Out of the hundreds of times I've babysat, most kids are fun to hang out with, innocent, a little scared of me at first and then by two or three visits so happy to see me they wave goodbye to Mommy and Daddy as soon as I walk through the door.

My friends ask me how I can love babysitting when I already have six little brothers and sisters and one older sister. Like I said, babysitting is about getting away from my screwed up parents, and about getting away from what they pass out to their kids. When I babysit I can be with kids who are not like my brothers and sisters. I get to visit other families and see how different it is when parents don't argue all the time with each other or their kids. I get to see what it's like to live in a house with only two children, where the kids are not told to shut up and sit down all the time, but spoiled with parents who are actually happy to have them. Babysitting is my escape into a different world where people appreciate me with money and thank-yous for at least a few hours.

Sometimes I feel like two different people. One person inside of me says "GET AWAY!" The other person says "Stay and protect your little sisters and brothers." Then I think what can I possibly do to stop my father and mother? As kids we have all learned to either shut up and take it or fight like my twelve year old brother Louis. The one problem these days is that Louis bullies the littler ones like Susan, Martha and Tina. Susan and Tina are protected from any real danger because one is my mother's pet (Susan) and the other (Tina) is my father's pet as long as they continue to play the shut-up-and-take-it game. Martha, though, is lost with no one to help her. So in a way, I feel like I adopted my little sister a few years ago. I told her to tell me if anyone like Louis is picking on her. I played games

14

with her, read stories with her and talked to her. She and I both weighed nine pounds and one ounce at birth, almost seven years apart to the day. She and I both had these scary looking birthmarks that shrunk and turned from fresh bruise-colored to skintone as we grew out of childhood. She and I are buddies.

Martha, along with my own bedroom downstairs and a chance to borrow the car from my mother are the main reasons I guess I don't run away from home. In short spurts, the bullshit is tolerable. Kind of like classes at school with teachers who annoy me. I tell myself "Whatever it takes to get a good grade, even if it means pretending to be fascinated with what they teach, I'll do it." The main goal at school and at home is to get out of there eventually, and I can play all the good girl games necessary to get what I want.

Two months after my seventeenth birthday, I auditioned for varsity cheerleading in the spring of my junior year in high school. It was Holy Thursday, three days before Easter Sunday, 1976.

"Fire up, fire up, up, up.
Fire up, fire up, up, up.
Sparks are flying 'cause we are tryin'
To fire up, fire up, up, up!"

Those were the final lines I performed in front of the panel of five judges and a couple hundred pep club members seated on gymnasium bleachers. My friend Chuck who was president of Pep Club kept his promise to root for me from the beginning. As I began I could hear people snickering in the audience. I was not your typical looking cheerleader. Five foot eight inches tall, 160 pounds, my parents' rather short yet sturdy limbs and my father's solid, square shaped head. Short brown hair with hazel eyes and very little sense of style compared to the other girls trying out. I had no confidence about my physical

Ann Kronlage

beauty but I did have a love of dance and movement in rhythm. I focused on some girl's purse that rested at eye level. I continued on with a gymnastics movement. I could hear the surprise in some voices when I finished with relative grace. Chuck was joined by the excited applause of many as I sat down.

As I returned to my seat on the gymnasium floor, next to the other sophomore and junior girls who had tried out just before me, a few hands patted me on the shoulders with "Good job." whispered in my direction.

I found out I made the squad the next day on Good Friday. I floated home with giddiness. A jury of my peers actually voted me in as good enough for varsity cheerleading. Amazing.

Five girlfriends and I made plans to go out the next evening. I only had to convince my parents to let me use the family station wagon.

"I'll clean the kitchen, dining room, and living room!" I bargained with my mother.

"One Flew Over The Cuckoo's Nest is playing at the movies." Rebecca said when we talked on the phone that night. "After that, we can go visit Mark Holtmeyer's. I heard he's having a party, and his mom will be gone all night. There should be a lot of guys there!" One of the best things about being Rebecca's friend was she always seemed to have the scoop on the action in our neighborhood. Rebecca, Sue, Tracey, Jane, Laura, and I agreed to go to the movie and to check out the party at Mark's.

My father, still gone at work, left the keys to the car in his dresser drawer, with instructions for me to take them out only after I finished my cleaning. Vacuuming and scrubbing clean every part of the kitchen and den was always a sure bet to get the car from my mother for a Saturday night.

"That was such a sad movie." Tracey said in the car as I drove the six of us out of the parking lot.

"I didn't want Jack Nicholson to die. What was the point of him dying?" Laura asked.

"We talked about this in Literature class." Rebecca spoke confidently. "It's like when Romeo and Juliet die at the end. Death always symbolizes the end of something; not necessarily a person's life, but maybe the end of that bitch Nurse Ratchett's reign as ice queen. You know?" She let out a quick laugh. I laughed too. That was the thing about Rebecca, she could always get me to laugh. Even when it seemed like she should be crying, she was laughing. Even when people laughed at her for not being a homecoming queen type of girl, Rebecca would hold her head high and make a clever joke.

"It's right here!" Rebecca screamed.

As I pulled the car into Mark's driveway, we each took a deep breath as we imagined the boys that were inside. Mark was one of the track jocks we all knew from practice after school. Seeing them at a party was a little scarier than on the track field in the middle of the day. "Be brave and take a chance." I told myself.

One of Mark's friends, Jim, answered the door, obviously happy to see us. He had a nice athletic body, with broad shoulders and a tight butt. His big brown, sad puppy dog eyes looked into mine and asked me if I wanted a beer. "Sure." I said, even though I didn't like the taste of beer. Several track jocks draped themselves on old chairs scattered around the unfinished basement. Music shouted across the room from an old stereo system. These guys all seemed as clueless as I did about the opposite sex. I felt better.

Jim tried to be cool and pay attention to us but you could tell he was enjoying being immature with the other guys. One of them started throwing wads of paper at another one. Pretty soon it was like a food fight with all of them getting into it. They laughed and acted funny like they were nervous. I was sure they were laughing at me. Rebecca began talking to Jim like she didn't feel nervous. How did she do that?.

Ann Kronlage

Suddenly Jim stood before everyone and announced "I'll bet you I can get all the beer out of this unopened can without popping the tab." Some of us bet he couldn't. Before anyone could think too long, he held an unopened can upside down, stabbed the bottom, held his finger against that hole, then stabbed another hole in the side. Beer froth dripped slowly down his forearms and he put his mouth against the side hole and sucked as if it were a girlfriend's mouth while he took his finger off the other hole. We all groaned and cheered as he stood there, grinning at having won the bet.

As our curfews approached, my five friends and I said goodbye and climbed into the car. Jim asked if he could come along and get dropped back to Mark's on my way home. I agreed since I knew it would tease my girlfriends' curiosity after they got dropped off and it gave me an excuse to drive around more.

After I dropped everyone off and Jim was the only one left, I pulled into Mark's driveway for the second time that night. As I backed out, after Jim walked across the hood of the old station wagon then through Mark's door, Keith, another guy from the party, stood alone with beer in hand, under the light of the full moon and waved good-bye.

I woke up laying down in a dark, speeding car. A woman's calm but serious voice above my face said to me, "You're very brave." as she gently stroked my forehead with what felt like her hand. Everything was dark except for the streetlights that reached in and out as we moved past them. A loud siren nearby sounded like we were racing an ambulance down the road. The woman repeated the same words and the same touch every fifteen seconds. I wanted her to stop and I wanted her to never stop.

"Where am I?" I asked her.

"You are in an ambulance on your way to the hospital." She said.

COOL! I felt for a second until I felt like I was going to throw up every time the car turned a corner.

"Can you ask the driver to slow down on the turns?" I whispered to her.

The next turn was slower and I didn't feel like throwing up anymore. I felt very tired and achey all over, but I still felt the excitement of riding in an ambulance that raced down the road! Ambulances and hospitals seemed like the most exciting places in the world to me—where miracles happened. Where people were born, where people died and where people were saved. In that moment I was one of the lucky ones being saved! How much more exciting could a person's life get?

As quickly as the ambulance raced down the road, it stopped. The engine turned off, the doors next to me opened and somebody pulled me out by the gurney underneath me. The frame of the gurney snapped into a raised position and somebody began pushing me like they do on my favorite TV show, <u>Medical Center</u>. Even with my eyes closed, I could tell we went from dark night to the annoying fluorescent brightness of inside. Even after I got used to the bright lights, I couldn't see —my glasses were missing. Where are my glasses? Why would anyone take my glasses?

I squinted and searched the hallway that my gurney was moving through. There was a woman sitting on a chair against the wall. I wondered what she was waiting for. I knew she was the mother or the wife of some patient inside somewhere. I looked into her eyes for some clue as my gurney passed. She looked at my eyes and drew in a loud, frightened gasp. My gurney kept moving and I wondered what was so horrifying about the way I looked.

My gurney continued on and I heard the rolling frame beneath me become muffled and noticed the blurry floor change pattern from an off-white linoleum to a large emerald green and navy blue leaf patterned carpeting. The gurney slowed and a male person with a bright orange T-shirt walked up to my side.

"Ann, it's Jim." he whispered. It was Jim, the friend I had taken along in my car that night, as I drove my girlfriends home. I wondered why he had come to the hospital since we weren't close friends. I opened my mouth to talk to him but only a whisper came out of me. I felt like I had just finished a long run on the track and could barely stay awake. "Bye." Came out of my mouth when I noticed my gurney continued down the hallway.

I awoke a second time, still on my back, to the sounds and blurred faces of my mother and father. My mother sobbed without words while my father sternly said, "You went out with Rebecca tonight when you told us you weren't going to!" I could feel my eyes pop open in surprise, as I imagined a severe punishment in my future.

My father didn't say anything for a moment, then spoke with a shaky voice. "As soon as you get out of here, we're gonna buy you a brand new car. Everything's gonna be okay."

A brand new car?! These words from my father's mouth were unbelievable, confusing, and wonderful at the same time.

I awoke a third time, again flat on my back in a brightly-lit room, with several people pushing and pulling at me. I lifted my head and saw a pair of female hands cut and remove my underpants. As I laid my head down again, I felt a new rush of the exhaustion and throbbing ache I had in the ambulance. Arms reached under my back and lifted me to a seated position. Dizziness added to the tired ache. A man's voice from behind me spoke loudly.

"Ann, can you hear me?" his voice was a pounding echo to my ears.

I nodded my drooping head.

"Ann, can you tell me how old you are?" he roared.

"Seventeen", I struggled to produce a sound louder than a whisper.

"Ann, can you tell me your birthday?"

I became annoyed at this third loud question. I wanted to tell him to talk quieter, but the words seemed trapped inside me.

"Two, sixteen, fifty nine", I replied.

"Ann, is this a birthmark?" he asked as I felt someone touching my back at my right shoulder blade. I nodded. The man seemed satisfied with my answers and the arms brought me back to a lying down position.

People hovered around me and spoke in medical terms I couldn't understand. Hands ripped open endless packages of waxy paper while frantic footsteps rushed in and out of the room. It smelled like a hospital—a dry tightness in the air. One or two different voices called to the outside of the room and asked if the OR was ready. A man spoke softly to another from the doorway.

"What happened to her?"

"Electrical burn." another man answered.

Electrical burn?! I thought. What the hell is an electrical burn?

I lifted my left hand close to my nearsighted eyes to see if there was some clue to be found. My arm, swollen and red, looked like a rubber body part from a Halloween display. My fingers curled in unnaturally. Around my wrist it looked as if my metal watch had melted an inch or two into my skin. I suddenly felt nauseous and scared and wanted to believe that this was all a bad dream.

Time froze and my mind raced through the shadows of my memory for clues to what had happened as my gurney was pushed out into a dark hallway and parked against the wall.

Ann Kronlage

"Please, put me to sleep!" I pleaded in the direction of the retreating transporter.

"The OR's almost ready, it won't be long." a female voice said cheerily as she walked away, as if this was good news.

"Please!" I struggled to be heard, "put me to sleep!"

No one answered this time. A dark, eerie silence grew louder with each passing second. This couldn't be real. I had been thrown into a dark, cold well and someone had just closed the lid.

My mother asked an attending nurse for a prognosis after I was admitted. The nurse responded, "Oh, she'll live through the night." With that news, my parents waited in the lobby of the large hospital as night became morning, and I was transferred from operating room to Burn Unit. My little brother Louis, twelve at the time, remembers waking up that morning to an unusual silence in our house where eight children and two parents lived. Eight Easter baskets were carefully filled to the brim and placed in a row the night before by my mother. Before she and my father were called to meet me at the hospital. As people all over the world celebrated Easter, a holiday marked with hope and renewal, my family and friends prayed.

In The Wake Of Shock

My friend Sandi got a great deal on a one week stay in Freeport, Bahamas and she invited me along and of course I accepted. Scuba diving was always a great excuse to take a vacation. Sandi and I met two years earlier, on Cayman Brac, on a dive that was my first after getting classroom instruction, and not her first, with her boyfriend Dave.

We signed up for diving as soon as we arrived at the hotel. The next morning we took off with a group of people we didn't know, to waters where we had never been. But that's the way it was with diving, as long as you had your buddy to dive with, you felt safe.

"It's not deep, but you'll have more time down to explore and the sunlight is direct so you can see everything better." The divemaster announced as he dropped anchor. As Sandi and I descended 25 feet to the bottom, I relaxed knowing it wasn't as dangerous at a shallow depth. There were lots of coral, fish and time to enjoy an easy dive.

After about 50 minutes, Sandi signaled that her air had reached 500psi. Mine was almost there too. We began to ascend when I noticed the faint sound of a boat motor in the distance. Underwater it is impossible to tell from which direction sounds originate. There was no mistaking though that the boat was getting louder and thus bigger with every few seconds. At about ten feet from the surface we turned to one another and made eye contact as if to say Do you hear that? Sandi motioned that she wanted to take off her vest and tank and let it float to the top like a buoy to tell the approaching boat we were down here. I motioned that we should go down to the deepest, closest spot we could find. She joined me after I began descending to a sink-hole at the sandy bottom. The boat motor got louder and louder fast. I laid myself flat on my stomach on the bottom, digging my fingers into the sand, and looking up, waiting and wondering Where is that boat? Within about a minute, a huge, speeding white hull cut through the water's surface 15 feet deep, directly above us.

As soon as it was obvious there were no other boats coming, we moved up to the surface and found our way to the boat waiting for us. Our divemaster helped us out of the water as he excitedly asked "Did you see that million dollar yacht go by?"

We both nodded in disbelief of what we had just experienced. We never went diving with that group again.

I woke up in a dark, cloudy room with beeping and breathing machine noises around me. I had a mask on my mouth and nose. Someone found my glasses and had put them on, though they weren't very useful since the mask made steam that kept them constantly fogged over. My body ached like a swollen mummy. Like someone had attached an air pump to my mouth and filled me to blimp capacity. I heard someone walk near my bed. The ache dripped out of my arms and I floated away.

I woke up to see several men in white coats, standing at the foot of my bed. Somebody had turned on the lights and taken the fog mask off my face. They whispered to one another and glanced at my bandaged feet.

"Ann, my name is Dr. Wray, I am one of the plastic surgeons taking care of you here at the hospital." He paused "Do you understand you are in a burn unit for electrical burns you sustained thirty six hours ago?"

I nodded even though I had no idea how long it had been

Ann Kronlage

since the ambulance ride.

"Ann, we're going to have to amputate the lower part of your left leg." Dr. Wray said slowly and gently.

WHAT???? My brain said. WHAT THE HELL IS HE TALKING ABOUT? "Why?" I heard my quivering voice ask.

"Because the tissue has been irreparably damaged and there's no circulation. When we made an incision along the length of your leg, there was no bleeding from the calf down. You can't move your left ankle."he said.

"Look, I can move it!" My brain was ready to jump off the roof of the Empire State Building or out of a 747 jet to prove to this man that he didn't need to amputate my leg. I rolled my left leg from side to side to show him he was wrong.

"I'm talking about the point and flex movement in your left ankle." he explained in a gentle voice.

I tried to move my foot at my ankle, but it stayed stiff like a mannequin. I stared at his eyes and saw that he was serious about cutting off my leg.

"Why do you have to do it now?" I asked, wondering how he could be so sure about it.

"We can wait, but you may develop gangrene in your leg, and that will cause us to have to amputate more. Right now we estimate that about ten inches of your leg will have to be amputated. We won't know for sure until we examine it closely on the operating table. We believe your knee can be saved now, but if we wait, that might not be the case."

The dizziness in my head felt like when I got hit in the back of the head with a baseball bat. It happened on the border between my family's backyard and the next door neighbor's backyard, when I was about 11 or 12. Bobby Rector, who lived next door, loved to practice his swings with a tethered baseball and a Louisville slugger. He wasn't expecting anyone to get too close and I wasn't expecting his bat to reach so far. Thunk! I sat then laid back in the soft plush grass of summer. I could see stars in the blue afternoon sky and in the dark of my closed eyes. It was a calm dizziness though. I didn't wonder if everything would be okay.

Sitting in the hospital bed, Dr. Wray's words were the Louisville slugger to my head. I was already down and there were no stars to be seen. I escaped with my new best friend, morphine.

I knew the morphine was wearing off again. Someone pushed me in a gurney down a concrete hallway. Grey, unfinished concrete, like a dungeon. My father walked alongside, dressed in his church clothes—a tie with a nice shirt and pants and his tan trenchcoat.

"I told Dr. Wray he couldn't amputate unless there was a damn good reason." He tried to sound tough. It was like somebody had pulled my eyelids open for the first time in my life. My dad had been scared a lot when I thought he was just mad.

He didn't want to say goodbye. "Don't you worry, everything's gonna be okay." He said, trying to sound like he knew what he was talking about. He wrinkled his forehead as they pushed me away.

Men and women with green masks and scrubs surrounded me, preparing for amputation without talking. Big bright lights invaded the space that wasn't filled by green. A tight odor like rubbing alcohol hung in the air. It matched the tightness of the people around me. I shivered.

I looked down at my arm with an IV sticking out of it as someone taped it to a board. I imagined Jesus Christ lying next to me, holding the hand on that arm. I knew he would stay there as long as I needed him. As the warmth of anesthesia began flowing first down my arms and then up my neck, I thought maybe they wouldn't have to take ten inches of my leg.

Maybe they would only cut it off at the ankle.

The next time I woke up I was back in the burn unit in my bed, still feeling like someone had beat the shit out of me. Then I remembered—my leg. What happened to my leg? I looked down at the covers over my legs. I picked them up. Like getting the gift you didn't want but expected, I looked at the swollen end bandaged up in white gauze rolls. It was as big as a head. It looked like they had amputated what they said they would—ten inches of my leg. My eyes told me it was gone but the feeling inside my leg told me it was still there. A tingling pins and needles feeling ran up my leg in a screw-like motion, like the stripes on a barber pole. Not a sharp pain really, just annoying. Like my leg was reeling from what just happened. What have you done to me? it would say if it could.

A nurse told me that whenever I wanted more morphine, as long as two hours had passed since the last dose, I could ring the bell (which she placed on my bed table) and get another dose of the stuff they seemed so eager to put into my IV. I could handle escaping to la-la land as much as I wanted and not thinking about what my leg looked like under the bandages.

What was really my life now was too much to believe. Wasn't this a bad dream, a nightmare? The morphine kept me in a fog enough that I held on to the fantasy that maybe this was all a nightmare, soon to be over. Each time a nurse gave me an injection into my IV, my mind and body floated. How could anything that felt so wonderful as this not be more real than the dark cave of knowing that my body was in big trouble? I couldn't remember how the trouble started but it was bad enough to get me a ride in a speeding ambulance, a stranger to gasp at the sight of me, my father to promise me a new car, and the lower ten inches of my leg amputated. It was a game of you keep giving me that stuff that feels so good and I won't ask questions or cause any trouble. I was willing to play that game for a long time.

Sometimes when I wake up, my dad is there looking sad and tender, like he's telling me how sorry he is for what happened. He and everybody who comes into my room has a surgical gown on backwards on top of their regular clothes. I hear him say he is sorry for being an asshole of a father for years and years. After that, drifting away to sleep is like a gentle dream on a soft, fluffy cloud. Sometimes my mom is there, crying non-stop. My sister Marie comes with her and stares into my eyes with her watery ones. My little brother P.J. came once but kept his head down and paced. My dad told me P.J. felt sick and left before everyone else that day. I never stayed awake long enough to talk with any of them. I closed my eyes in the middle of the noise pollution coming out of their mouths and they would walk away or stop talking without any argument. I said shut up without really saying it and everybody did what I wanted them to do. Incredible.

Lights turn on. Bright, fluorescent, annoying, pain-inducing lights. I imagined a blown fuse somewhere that would cause a power failure in my room.

"Hi Ann, it's Dottie", said a quiet voice. I opened my eyes to see a pretty, petite, blond-haired, blue-eyed woman with a gentle smile.

"Hi", I scratched. My throat felt like sandpaper. "Can I take a nap, you know, can you give me some morphine to help me sleep?"

"We can no longer give you morphine, Ann, you've been taking it now for two weeks and the policy of this hospital is no addictive drug will be continuously given for a period beyond two weeks. It's to protect you from becoming addicted, which you wouldn't want to happen."

I wanted to grab her skinny little white neck till she begged for morphine so I could spit her words back at her.

Telling me no more morphine was like telling me at four

years old there was no Santa. Like being left in the middle of the ocean right before a storm is ready to hit and not being able to swim. Dottie stood at the shore and yelled that she couldn't swim either.

"I'm sorry Ann, we just can't do it. I'll be around if you need anything else." She walked back to the nurses' station.

"My ass!" I said to myself. What the hell was I supposed to do now?

Some idiot who said he's the hospital psychologist comes to my room. "Ph.D." I read on his nametag as he blabbers on about something and squeezes his face into attempted understanding. "Phucking Dumbshit." I laugh to myself. He complimented me on how amazing I was to be able to smile at a time like this. Luckily, he started to squirm from being around me and made some excuse about having to leave. Extra luckily, he never came back.

A female about my age comes up to me with a tray of food. She puts it on my table, then without a word, walks away. Nice to meet you too Miss Hairnet. I read the card sitting on top. "Your lunch for today is…" then choices made by somebody I never talked to are checked. Macaroni and cheese, green beans, applesauce, milk, orange juice and a piece of chocolate cake with icing. They looked good but I wasn't even in the mood to eat. That's something I had never experienced before, not wanting to eat.

Before being in the hospital, I probably had what some people would now call an eating disorder. Very seldom did I feel truly hungry, and often I had indigestion. I ate too much at home, usually when I was pissed off at my mother for telling me I needed to lose weight, or because she hid the store-bought cookies and cupcakes from my older sister Marie and I. When I found the hidden sweets or got mad enough at her, I devoured as much as I could as quickly as I could. I thought of her determination to control me as I bit, chewed and gulped every bite.

Eating too much became the best way I knew how to get back at her for thinking she could tell me what to do. She wanted a slender daughter, so I would give her a fat one. I didn't even enjoy the taste of the forbidden cookies, just the thought of revenge on my mother.

I thought of a snake that I saw in my biology class. Before it could eat its prey, it had to feel safe enough in the environment to unlock its jaw. Unlocking the jaw puts the snake in a very vulnerable position, so eating is a big deal, not something done on impulse. I was like a snake looking around my strange environment, not feeling safe, not ready to eat.

Dottie walked up to me with two little paper cups in her hand. "These are your pain pills and these are pills you need to take with each meal. This antacid you also need to take with each meal." Eight pills, liquid chalk and an appetite still asleep. What more did I need to give me reason to eat?

"I really don't feel like eating." I said. If she knew the old me, she'd be laughing at those words coming out of my mouth.

"It's very important that you eat, Ann, if you want to heal. And if you want to get out of here." Those words got my attention. I did want to get out of there.

"Okay." Dottie pushed some button and my electric bed sat me up straight. I tried to make friends with the food on the tray that Dottie put in front of me. Compared to the cafeteria food at school, this stuff looked good.

"Can you hold the fork?" Dottie asked. What a stupid question, I thought. Holding the fork with my right hand was easy. "Now with your left hand." She said.

My left hand was a different story. It was the first thing I remember in the emergency room that really scared me. It didn't move like my left hand used to, like my right hand still did. I couldn't feel pain, just numbness. Swollen stiff numbness. My arm was wrapped like a mummy with rolls of gauze bandages.

Only my stiff fingers lay exposed. They look so tired from trying to move and confused from not being able to move. It was weird to look at my hand, tell it to move and nothing happened. Like when Dr. Wray told me my left ankle couldn't move and I looked at it, told it to move and it didn't. So bizarre.

I ended several minutes of trying to hold a fork by weaving the handle of the fork over and under the fingers on my left hand. I had outsmarted her, I told myself, and that told me that they didn't have all the answers. She looked disappointed but had to admit I was holding the fork with my fingers, just like she requested.

"When you're finished, ring the bell and I'll come get the tray."

"What's an electrical burn?" I asked Dottie before she got away.

"It's a burn that happens from electric current."

"Do you know what happened to me?" I asked.

"Yes, but I think you should talk to your mother, who will be here any minute." She looked nervous all of a sudden. "Visiting hours are from 12 to 1 and she's been coming every day, sometimes with your sister. Ring me if you need something. See ya." She escaped in her tiny, squeaky nurse's shoes.

My mother and sister Marie walked in. Marie looked around my sparse little room, avoiding eye contact with me, while my mother looked wiped out on two legs. Both of their faces struggled to offer me a smile. "They said you're awake now." My mother said with propped up hope, like I was a young child she could convince.

"You really should eat." My mother said as she looked at my tray of hospital lunch. What a bizarre thing to hear come out of her mouth. Years earlier, my mother once sat Marie and I down at the kitchen table and told us we needed to start enjoying cottage cheese. She placed a bowl in front of my sister, filled it halfway with cottage cheese and stuck a spoon in it. Marie wrinkled her nose. I got my own bowl of curdled milk and spoon put in front of me.

"Now eat it!" she said like it was a real emergency. Like the world was gonna stop if we didn't eat that shit she knew we didn't like. We sat there and stared at our bowls of curds for about an hour till Mom got distracted. That was one guarantee in life —that Mom would find something else to worry about if you waited long enough.

It was almost funny having my mom tell me to eat more if it wasn't for my foot being chopped off and me feeling like crap.

"Why can't I see out of this eye?" I suddenly realized I couldn't see both Marie standing at the left side of my bed and my mother standing at the right side of my bed without turning my head.

My mother looked around the room. "You need a mirror. I'll go get you a mirror." She said, pleased to be able to do something. She walked forward from the door, toward the nurses' desk. Within a minute, she came back with a hand mirror. I took it from her and held it in front of my face. I searched for a moment to find something on this creature's face I could recognize.

"Oh my God." I said softly to myself. My right cheek was covered in white gauze bandage, my right eye was swollen shut and the left side of my face bulged in a desperate attempt to maintain a hold on what remained of my facade. I was a swollen freak. What a sad, odd and poignant sight I was. The only part of the reflection in the mirror I recognized was my left eye. It twinkled with a loving and determined look at me. I'm in this with you, for the long haul, it seemed to say.

"What happened to me?" I asked.

My mother's face melted into a blob of tears on soft, white cheeks. "Oh Gussie!" she sobbed, pulled a chair next to my bed and gently put her hands on the edge of my mattress. "I'm so sorry." More sobbing.

I cried seeing her cry. I cried because it scared me to see everyone around me scared. I cried because it seemed like all I could do.

"I'm so sorry this happened." she said with a wet face. I imagined her saying I'm so sorry I was a bad mother all these years. I'm sorry I made you feel like a useless excuse for a daughter. I'm sorry I ignored you. I'm sorry I didn't appreciate you for being alive and being my daughter. I cried because I heard all those apologies in her tears.

It felt weird crying with my mother. Usually I refused to let her ever see me cry. It was something we never talked about but we all knew crying, or any kind of expression was just something you never did in our house. My dad ridiculed "crybabies" or "smart alecks" (anyone with an opinion different from his) so we all became conditioned like Pavlov's dog to maintain a blank expression in front of the two people we supposedly came from. So crying with or in front of my mother was so strange I couldn't do it for very long without wanting to tell her to shut up and find her own soap opera to cry about. She was actually pretty good at that, finding her own soap operas. She fell asleep to them every afternoon. They lulled her to sleep like morphine did for me.

I ran out of tears before she did. I needed to know what I was crying about. "What happened to me?" I asked again.

"You were at your friend Mark's house. Do you remember? You pulled out of his driveway. An electric line fell on your car. They yelled at you to stay in the car but you got out and that's when you were shocked. They gave you CPR. Those boys saved your life Gussie." She let out some air and cried again.

She told me stuff I couldn't imagine really happening. If that really happened, why couldn't I remember it? Like the rest of me, my mind moved slow with understanding this craziness my mother described.

"Dad will come at supper time. He's trying to get one of the boys who was there to visit and explain to you what they remember."

"I'm sorry, but visiting hour is over. You can come back at dinner time if you'd like." Dottie said to my mother and sister.

"Okay." My mother said in her sheepish way, with a nervous giggle at the end. "I'll see you tomorrow." She moved toward me and realized any touch from her hands would probably hurt so she kissed me. Marie kissed my fat cheek too. In any other situation I would have been grossed out having my mother and sister kiss me but there in the burn unit, nothing was ordinary.

Five hours later, right after they tried to convince me to eat dinner, my father did visit with Jim, as in Jim who was there when I don't remember what happened happened. "You remember Jim, Gussie? He's come here to tell you what he remembers." My father pulled up a chair to the foot of my bed and turned on my electric bed so my back was raised to a seated position. "Are you okay?" he asked, touching the edge of my mattress and looking at me with gentle eyes. "I'll come back in a little while." He said after I nodded okay. Jim sat in the chair and my father stepped out of the room.

"Do you remember anything about that night?" Jim asked shyly with big, brown, nervous eyes.

"The last thing I remember was you walking across the hood of my car to get inside Mark's house." I said. Jim blushed and smiled.

"Yeah, I was pretty drunk that night. But I did make it down the stairs. A few minutes later, Keith was flashing the lights on and off and yelling at Mark, Greg and I to come upstairs, NOW! We went upstairs and saw your car had hit a pole and a live wire was sparking a lot and bouncing off the back of your car. You were still half on, half off the car, with your face on the ground. For some reason, you stepped out of the passenger side of the station wagon, instead of the driver's side. Keith and Greg ran around the yard then inside the house to find something wooden to pull you off with." He took a deep breath and looked sad, then took another breath. "I couldn't just let you lay there, so I squatted down and pulled you by the armpits. I was thrown about ten feet across the yard! It didn't hurt and boy did I sober up fast. I stood back up and tried again, that time getting you off from contact with the car. I laid you on your back. You weren't breathing and you didn't have a pulse. Keith and I did CPR. Mark was inside calling the ambulance. They arrived after you started breathing." He stared at me with disbelief in recalling the whole story.

"Wow." I said softly. "Thank you for doing that for me." I felt so special for being saved but so crappy at the same time.

"Anybody would have done it." He said shyly. "How are you doing?"

"I don't know." I said. "I don't feel so great and they just cut off my leg so I don't know right now I guess."

"There were so many people at school asking about you that a bunch of us: Rebecca, Laura, Jane, Sue, Keith, Greg, Mark and me skipped classes one day and all got detention together the next Saturday. The girls brought some crayons and coloring books and colored the whole time. Don't tell anybody, but some of us guys did too." He laughed and I smiled.

Then there was an uncomfortable silence until my father walked in and said that they had to leave, that visiting hour was over. He told me he would see me tomorrow at visiting hour. They both said if I needed anything to just ask, then said good-bye and walked out.

I lay awake for a long time that night, wondering how something like the story Jim just told me could be real. Yet when I saw my unbandaged body there was no doubt it had happened. It was exhilarating to imagine myself as the heroine of some unbelievable story as if I turned the pages, read the words, studied the illustrations and lived the journey all at the same time.

Ann Kronlage

Adrift

The final part of my certification as a scuba diver, after classroom lectures, written tests and pool practice was to go to open water and complete certain maneuvers. The open water I chose was Cayman Brac in the Caribbean. Cayman Brac was a beautiful little island just south of Cuba, one of the three Cayman Islands of which Grand Cayman is the most famous. You can have the popular islands, I say, and give me a quiet, small island that doesn't have miles of hotels and restaurants but does have some of the most pristine, unspoiled waters and reef around. "Dive, Eat, Sleep." is what one diver's t-shirt had on it. That was the ideal schedule of a diver's vacation.

Night diving certification was an extra option that I signed on for one evening. My buddy Bob, an older man who wasn't much for conversation or friendly connection, felt more like an annoying distraction than an accomplice in a new adventure. My classroom instructor Bob and his girlfriend Judy would descend with us so I assumed that would even out my uneasy feelings.

The red light from a distant setting sun was just leaving the horizon as we descended into the dark water, from the brightly lit boat driven by Gregory, who lived on Cayman Brac all his life. He must have been thinking let the foolish Americans learn the hard way. We each turned our flashlights on, making things a little friendlier. I let the air out of my vest to help my body go down but noticed the distance between me and the others increasing. They were going down and I was going nowhere it seemed. Or were they going in a horizontal direction? Where was up? Where was down? Everything was dark and quiet except for the sound of my breathing, which was like a Darth Vader noise. I felt the surface of the water hit my back. I had gone up instead of down. I looked below for the lights of the two Bobs and Judy and saw they were about fifty feet away underwater and not even noticing what happened to me! I stuck my head out of the water. Recorded music bellowed from the dive boat that swayed with the waves in the distance, a greater distance than going below, so I chose down as my direction once again. Within five or ten minutes I caught up to them. They continued on with me in tow, never noticing I had been gone. Their focus was on a beautiful rainbow fish. A dreary brown, speckled color until it moved and its side fins spread out like bird's wings, like accordion folded fans colored the spectrum of a vivid rainbow. Its beauty could not be seen so well under the diffused light of day as under the sharp illumination of artificial light. Sights like that were the treasures of night diving, I would realize later.

Instructor Bob took pictures with his expensive underwater camera, noted the time and his gauge telling him air was getting to 500psi, looked at each of our gauges, which read fairly similar, then gave us the thumbs up sign. We ascended to a dark surface, with the boat now twice as far as it had been when I saw it before.

We each attempted to swim in the direction of the boat, whose music was blaring so loudly there was no chance we could yell or blow our whistles to get Gregory's attention. We were no match for the powerful sea. It was obvious we would get nowhere trying to pull our heavily-geared bodies through the water. Bob said we were too low on air to waste it on going ten feet lower and swim less restricted toward the boat. The real problem, Bob confessed then, was that we had gone against one of the basic rules of diving, swim out against the current, in with the current. I couldn't believe I had trusted this man to know what he was doing! I held back my anger, behind the urgency I felt about reaching the boat. What if we continued to drift till we could not be found? What if something below decided we were dinner?

Eventually Gregory turned on the boat's headlights and slowly moved the boat in the direction he knew we had gone. We were lucky to have an experienced man like him on board. I hauled myself up the ladder onto the boat, saltwater spilling off my body as "Goddammit!" spat out of my mouth. I didn't know what to do with my feelings of fear, betrayal and anger.

Why couldn't I just go to sleep till this was all over? I felt like Jack Nicholson's character in One Flew Over The Cuckoo's Nest. He found himself in a bizarre hospital ward, where everyone behaved as though the abnormal was normal. Swallow this, do that, and don't expect to get what you want because you are now under the control of hospital policy. Like it or not.

At the same time, it was cool to be in the middle of an ICU. I always loved watching Medical Center on TV because everyone rushed around with injured or sick patients, helping them live and sometimes watching them die. I loved that drama of the human spirit.

Dottie came into my room again to check my heart monitor.

"Why is a partition wall there?" I asked, pointing toward the wall to the right of me.

"You're in the corner of the burn unit where only survivors of burns stay. There are four other burn patients in here and they all happen to be men—Jim, Quinn, Isaac and Floyd, so we thought you'd appreciate the privacy."

The kitchen girl who came and picked up my lunch tray of untouched food looked the same age as me. I asked her what day it was. "Tuesday." She said to me with a confused look on her face. She spun around and rushed out of the room as if afraid of me.

I want to get out of here but the only way I can is to put up with this place for six more weeks, according to Dr. Wray. He also told me, "If I had to pick a perfect age for what happened to you, so that your chances of recovery were the greatest, it would be the age you are now." He spoke like a proud father. That was pretty cool. I was one of those amazing cases like on Medical Center.

"There's a sixty-five year old patient named Isaac who's been in here for six months!" said Liz, another nurse.

"How did he get burned?" I asked.

"He was minding his son's liquor store. Working the cash register, when some doped up robber came in and fired a blowtorch at his face." Liz stopped.

"My God." I said.

"You'll see him walking by." Liz said. "It is truly amazing to see what people can survive. You too Ann. And you have a young body on your side. Isaac wasn't expected to survive but *Isaac* expected to survive. That makes all the difference. Before you know it six weeks will be up. Think of Isaac when it seems tough." Liz was so sure, I had to believe her.

Liz looked about the same age as my mother but tall and thin with long limbs and fingers unlike my mother's short, round body with short limbs and fingers. My mother always seemed uncomfortable with her body, again the opposite of Liz, who traveled in her body like it was an old friend.

"Tell me about the other patients in here." I said to her.

"Well I would but I have to go now. Why don't you try to rest or watch some TV?" she said, looking around then pushing one on a wheeled cart in front of my bed.

Nothing but stupid soap operas. They're worse than sitting

here in the quiet. Quiet in my space anyway. Outside my room they're were phones ringing, the hospital p.a. system paging names every few minutes, other TVs blaring commercials, nurses talking, laughing and walking around between the other patients to the right of me and the office to the left of me. Mostly female nurses and male patients.

Dottie came in. "Ann, we need to weigh you." she said.

This should be interesting, I thought.

She stepped back as two men pushed in on wheels, a big hammock hanging from a steel frame. They lowered the hammock to my mattress and helped me scoot my butt and back onto it. The problem was my ass had only a sheet on it cause the paper thin gown I wore was too short to do the job. As I scooted, my hairy crotch peered out and the two men exchanged a smile which I caught but Dottie did not. Creepy jerks were more interested in copping a peek than helping me with my tired, bandaged body. The assholes had to be told to pull the sheet over. One of them pushed a button that lifted me up in the hammock.

"One hundred and ninety pounds." one of them said as Dottie wrote it down on a clipboard.

"One hundred and ninety pounds!" I blurted. "That can't be right. I weighed a hundred and sixty the last time I checked!"

"The thirty pounds is fluid retention all over your body. It's a normal reaction for your body to have after third degree burns. You'll lose it all and then some by the time you get out of here." Dottie said.

I looked at Dottie, who probably topped out at ninety five pounds on a scale. What did she know about gaining too much weight?

"You're burning 4000 calories a day just lying in bed, Ann. Trust me, you won't stay at a hundred and ninety pounds." she said in her gentle voice. "Even if you eat like a pig for the next six weeks." We both knew that wasn't going to happen, since all I wanted to do was gag at the thought of food. Okay, I can live with a hundred and ninety pounds for now.

The three of them left with the electric hammock.

"Hi Ann." A woman said as she walked into my room. She wore a white lab coat with regular clothes underneath. "I am an occupational therapist. I am going to help you with your range of motion." Her name was Marlene and she had just graduated from college which meant she was only five years older than me. She was shy but happy as she talked to me about the changes in my body, especially the places where I would have skin grafts and would need to do things to help my body heal the best way possible. "Let's start with your left hand." She gently held my stiff cold hand in hers. She didn't seem shocked by anything about me which made me like her instantly. I would see her again and again as I got better, always with a warm smile and friendly words of encouragement.

One evening Rebecca came to visit with my father. She had a school newspaper that mentioned my name in a little box in the center of one of the pages. "Ann Kronlage is listed in critical condition." Rebecca read.

"What?" I blurted out. My 17 year-old mind couldn't imagine that I was in such desperate shape.

"I'll talk to Dr. Wray." My father said, agreeing with me that I no longer merited critical status. I was quickly taken off the critical list, partly because the doctors knew that the power of suggestion was so great.

I wondered about my friends. They were at school, feeling sleepy, grumbling about Friday being so far away, and talking about who was dating who. Did they wonder about me? Did they miss me like I missed them?

A few minutes later, Dottie came in with a handful of mail all addressed to me! Cards mostly, with tons of names signed on them. Some names I didn't know, others I knew very well. Not a lot of messages to me directly though, besides "Get Well Soon!" or "Hang in there!" When you think about it what can a person say to someone like me? Some cards had letters with the latest gossip or what so and so did since I last saw them. In one instant, I floated in love for all of these friends sending their love, but felt so tired and isolated from knowing all of this happened to me alone.

Rebecca wrote, "The first day at school, after you went to the hospital, there was an eerie silence everywhere, even in the cafeteria. Everybody was stunned to hear what had happened to you." So weird. I was an absent celebrity in a school of 2000 kids! I wanted to skip class like Rebecca said a group of them did, as Jim had told me when he came to visit, out of frustration from being mobbed by people who asked them all week long what had really happened to me.

I pressed the buzzer at my right hand, the one someone told me to use to ask for help. This time not Dottie, but a man who reminded me of my sixth grade teacher, Mr. Tate, walked through my doorway.

"I'm Marvin." He said, just the way Mr. Tate spoke, in a slow monotone. He looked like Mr. Tate too, with straight sandy blonde hair that almost touched his stooped shoulders, and sleepy, big brown eyes.

"What did you need?" He droned. A little unfriendly like Mr. Tate too, I thought.

"Uh, I need to go to the bathroom." I felt my face blush with embarrassment.

"Just a minute." He said, then walked out toward the nurses station beyond where I could see him.

A heavy-set woman with white hair, a lot older than my mother, came in with a chrome bedpan in one hand and a roll of toilet paper in the other. She at least appeared friendlier than Marvin.

"Hi, I'm Delores. You need to use the bathroom?" She looked at me sweetly.

"I want to use the toilet, the kind that flushes." I said, hoping I wouldn't have to use that thing she held.

"We can't move you dear. You have no choice right now. Doctor says you can't be moved to go to the toilet. You might fall and break a bone." She waited as if it didn't matter to her what I said.

"I can't use a bedpan. I just can't." I told her. "Wait a minute, how did I pee before now?"

"You had a catheter in you before, but we took that out early this morning. Doctor says without the morphine you can handle peeing on your own." Delores seemed comfortable with the idea that someone knew what to do.

"Okay, well you let me know when you're ready." She said, again as if it didn't matter when or what I decided.

I imagined a conspiracy among the nurses telling me I had no other choice but a bedpan because they didn't want to bother dragging me to the toilet. I could barely sit up, much less drag myself to the toilet. Pissing in a bowl in bed? How could I do that? As I thought about it, my bladder grew more uncomfortable with each minute that passed.

Delores came back with the bedpan and toilet paper without a word, after I pressed the buzzer next to my bed.

She stood over me with the roll of toilet paper in her hand.

"I can't pee while you're standing there." I said to her.

"Oh, I'm sorry!" She sounded sincere and taken aback by a reminder that there was a person behind the body. She stepped out of the room till I let her know I needed her again.

Just as I wondered what would come next, Marvin appeared, and he didn't look any friendlier.

"It's time to change your bandages." He spoke like Delores had, as if I didn't have a choice in the matter. "You'll need to go next door where you can take a bath too."

Marvin lowered the left side of my bed and rolled a gurney against it and asked me to scoot onto its narrow platform. I slowly made my way across and Marvin told me to watch my fingers as he pushed me out the door, then to the left, then another left. We entered the room next to mine, on the other side of my left wall.

I scooted across to another gurney that had a turquoise-colored rubber skirt. Dottie came in and raised the rubber sides with one snap of the metal frame, converting my gurney to a bathtub. On the wall in front of me, I saw four faucets with green garden hoses attached to each, sprouting out about shoulder high to Marvin. Marvin brought the end of one hose to my bathtub and told me we would fill it after we removed my lower bandages. Dottie gave me a towel to cover my crotch. Marvin laid the hose beside me and turned on the water till I told him the temperature reached comfortable. He told me not to worry, that the water temperature could be adjusted.

Dottie laid out about twenty rolls of gauze and a fresh hospital gown on a table next to me.

"This will hurt." Marvin said while looking down at my foot and unrolling the length of gauze. Several layers of soft white gauze were quiet warning to what came next.

Gauze put on wet twelve hours earlier had become a stiff, unyielding cover to my open wounds. Where Marvin peeled the bottom layer of gauze, blood oozed and I grunted and gasped with clenched teeth. The sharp stinging pain grew like the roar of a giant beast ready to devour me. In the midst of such pain, all fears, worries and thoughts merge into one focus—how to make it stop. If I moved, Marvin stopped to explain to me why I shouldn't and it seemed an eternity before he shut up and began again. For some reason, the peeling could not take place under the water. The sooner he finished, I learned quickly, the sooner the stinging could be relieved by immersion in the bath water.

"This is specially treated water for you to soak in. It's sterilized and we add this silver sulfadiazine liquid to the water to coat your burns to keep out bacteria." He seemed awfully damn calm in the middle of this stinging that rose out of me like a blaring siren. Even with large doses of morphine in their bodies, burn patients, myself included, have been known to scream profanities at their caregivers as the lowest layer of gauze is peeled from raw tissue.

Once the water level rose above my legs, the pain went away, but the whole thing began again on my upper half. Fortunately, my right cheek received a skin graft while I slept through morphine, during one of the two operations the first few days I came to the burn unit.

The tissue on my arms, legs, and chest looked like raw hamburger meat. Dr. Ollinger, Dr. Wray's resident student, later told me the hamburger meat was the layer of fat we all have beneath multiple layers of skin. No scab would ever form and no skin would ever regenerate on this hamburger meat. Only future skin grafts from other parts of my own body would fix it. I didn't even recognize this body, this lack of skin that was now mine. I didn't feel or look like the person I last saw in the mirror.

No burns on any part of the back of my body, which meant I could at least sit or lay in bed without pressure on any open wound.

I watched my seventeen year old body with fascination, horror and intense compassion. For whatever reason, this body persevered through electric shock, amputation and now bandage changing. My body was my faithful companion and if it could go on, so could I.

For at least a week, my eyes told me the majority of my right breast was a lump of hamburger meat. I silently accepted the loss of my right nipple, afraid to ask any of the doctors or nurses about it. Compared to a foot, a nipple didn't seem so important. What's done is done, I told myself. Later, I noticed the bottom half of my right breast, including my nipple, had not disappeared under the wrath of electricity. "I thought my nipple had been burned away but didn't know what to say or do about it." I said to Liz. "Does that sound crazy?" I asked her.

"No." She answered softly with her head down.

Sometimes one or both nurses would walk out of the room after bandage removal and leave me to languish in warm, soothing bath water.

"Take your time" I would say to them as I closed my eyes and tried to remember what it felt like to have only "good" skin. Not good skin the way my friends would describe skin with no pimples and not good skin the way my mother would describe skin with no wrinkles. Just pain-free skin, with fine delicate hairs that miraculously held sweat glands beneath. Skin that I didn't have to think about, that became my new definition of good skin. With jealousy I noticed the undamaged skin on the nurses as they gently wrapped fresh gauze rolls, dipped in the bath water, around my arms, legs and chest. Once my open wounds had a warm wet layer over them, a fresh hospital gown found its way around me and I scooted my numbed body back onto the gurney that had brought me there.

Within a half-hour though, the warm wet layer cooled, and unless someone brought me warmed sheets, I began to shiver. During the first week after morphine withdrawal, I remained silent and shivered until the bandages air-dried, which took several hours. My mother noticed one day when she visited at lunch that I shivered. So much was happening to my body I didn't think that being cold was unnecessary and something about which I could complain. She went to the nurses and

immediately got warmed sheets to cover my wet bandages.
Several rounds of warmed sheets were required till my bandages
dried and I stopped shivering. That was the first time my
mother demonstrated to me how to advocate for myself. Before
then, before being a patient in an intensive care unit, it was
expected in our family, church and school that any discomforts
were better left quietly endured. It was an envied characteristic
in the Catholic mentality, to suffer silently and willingly before
a God that one also needed to fear because the threat of pain
as punishment also loomed. My experience with pain and
discomfort in the hospital would contradict many ideas in my
upbringing, certainly all for the better.

I hadn't watched when Marvin undressed my amputation
site. After seeing my arms uncovered, I didn't feel ready for
what I imagined an even more gruesome sight. A "stump" they
called it. I hated that word more each time I heard it.

"We took ten inches, but saved your knee." Dr. Wray told
me in an attempt to encourage me. I wanted Dr. Wray to tell
me they were able to save the whole leg. I wanted to tell everyone
I knew to appreciate their legs, strong or not, fast or not,
good-looking or not. It's the way my friends and I have always
felt about cars, cars we could use to go cruisin' in—as long as it
got us from here to there—that was a great car.

The only person I heard about having an amputated leg was
Totie Fields, a short, chubby standup comedienne I saw on
Johnny Carson. She had cancer which caused the reason for the
amputation.

"We were able to save your big toe on the remaining foot."
Dr. Wray said to me. "With that big toe, you'll have a much
easier time walking and balancing."

Was I supposed to be happy about that? It felt like Rebecca
telling me to say yes to Mike Layne, who asked me a month earlier
to go to prom, cause at least I'd be able to say I went. Even
though I didn't really like him—he was strange, weird, and

talked to me like he was reading from a script. Maybe it's just me, I thought, but I wished I could find a good enough reason to say "Sorry, but I'm busy that night." Now I had an unstoppable excuse to get out of going to prom with him, and I bet all the money in the world he wouldn't be bugging me to go anywhere with him anymore.

It must have been dinner time cause in walked my dad. He looked so shy in the yellow backwards gown every visitor had to wear over street clothes when coming into my space. He looked the way he did when he came to 7:30 Mass.

Before Catholic school began every weekday, two hundred of us were marched over to church where we sat in tight little groups according to our grade level. Visitors, my dad included, sat where they could in the back. Before he went to work he came to sit through the half hour service. I didn't look for him but knew he was there if he coughed. A gentle, respectful, thoughtful cough. I liked that dad who came to church before school.

I liked the dad who came to visit me in the Burn Unit everyday too. He wasn't his usual cocky, bully self. Like he knew he wasn't in charge anymore. Truth was he was never in charge except for in his own little mind. Amazing. I couldn't believe it. This person who was my father really didn't hate me if he bothered to come visit me everyday. He looked so sad, yet so proud, to see me like I was.

"You're so brave." He said with real admiration in his eyes.

If I wasn't so surprised, I would have cried with joy. This person I knew as an asshole bully pig was actually kind-hearted. My God.

"The doctors say you have been amazing. You're young and strong so you're gonna be okay. You're lucky to be alive." He sounded grateful to be able to say that.

"Do you remember that night at all?" He asked.

"I remember dropping Jim off and him walking across the

hood to get to Mark's door." I said.

"It looks like you have a strong lawsuit building against the electric company. It seems that high power line that fell when you barely bumped the pole was due for repair. They were negligent which means you could be rich in a few years." My father smiled with great pleasure at the thought of such a thing playing out before his eyes. "I'd let them cut off my leg for a million bucks. How about you Gussie?"

"I don't know. It's hard to say since it's already done for me. You know?" I said. My father laughed at me the way he did when he thought me a naïve little girl. I understood what he meant but I wasn't ready to admit that a million dollars was a fair trade for forty percent of my skin and ten inches of my leg.

Just then a tray of food arrived. Stuff that looked like food that used to taste good to me, but now was so boring. Along with six different pills and liquid chalk, how did they expect me to eat?

"Visiting hour is over, I'm afraid." Liz popped her head in the doorway and said to the both of us.

My dad got up to leave, but he didn't know how to say good-bye. He couldn't do what he normally did—ignore me without saying goodbye or slap me in a nervous, social imbecilic way he did at other times. He could only be genuine and say "I'll be back tomorrow at dinnertime. You're gonna be okay."

Later that evening, I noticed what felt like I had started my period. Right on schedule from when my last one had been, I thought to myself. I pushed my call button and in walked Becky, the head nurse of the burn unit. I explained to her that I had started my period and needed a pad.

"That's impossible. The menstrual cycle always stops for a few months after a trauma such as yours." She said in the curt manner she always spoke.

I held back my urge to laugh. She walked away quickly as if

to say that were the end of the discussion. I woke up later and noticed someone had put a pad under me while I slept. I believed her when she said it wasn't possible to menstruate and my body soon stopped doing so and didn't begin again for several months as it had been told.

I mentioned to both my mother and father that the head nurse Becky had something wrong with her. Telling me blood on my sheet was impossible. Becky really reminded me of Nurse Ratchett in One Flew Over The Cuckoo's Nest. My parents mentioned something to Dr. Wray and his response was that Becky was a very capable nurse and we shouldn't be concerned. I remember that was the attitude the doctors had about Nurse Ratchett too.

I turned on the television one day and saw Muhammed Ali being interviewed. I understood the persona he presented to the world both in and out of the ring. He wanted to remain undefeated and that required a display of invulnerability, unemotional strength, and constant vigilance toward his enemies. I felt that way in the burn unit; like a boxer poised for the fight. Like a gladiator who knows you either keep fighting or you die. I could only trust God and myself and at that point it didn't feel like God wanted to talk to me.

A few days later, I lifted myself into a wheelchair while Marvin, Dottie, and Kathy happily chatted away, changing my sheets, when a wave of dizziness hit me. I told them that I felt light-headed. They said I could lie down when they finished in a few minutes. I closed my eyes, hoping the dizziness would go away. It did, in fact I felt as though someone had injected morphine into me.

"Ann?" Dottie said loudly to me. I couldn't get my mouth to answer, it wouldn't work. Somebody grabbed my eyes, pulled the lids open, but I couldn't see, as if my eyes were still shut.

"She's fainted!" I heard Dottie say frantically. "I'll call Dr. Wray!"

I felt like I floated above it all, and had given my dizziness away; to Dottie, Marvin, Kathy, and those doctors on the phone. Such a wonderful, peaceful place, where nothing hurt and nothing mattered. "I'm right here!" I wanted to say, but nothing moved, like my brain no longer controlled my body.

"We have to move her back to bed!" Dottie yelled from the phone across the room.

"I'll lift her." Marvin's voice said from above me. I felt him bury his fingers and hands under my knees and behind my neck. He groaned as he tried to lift me, obviously having more trouble than he anticipated. In another place and time I would have panicked with embarrassment and fear to have some man struggle with my body, for fear that he might drop me, but not in that moment. I had one part of me in an invisible world where all was perfect and another part of me feeling the sensations of living in this completely relaxed body. With a few more grunts, he managed to get my limp dense body onto the bed a few feet away.

Dottie hung up the phone as she yelled across the room. "They said it's okay!"

"You're right." I wanted to say to Dottie, "It is going to be okay. Everything's going to be okay."

Skinned Alive

He didn't seem to notice how the sky and sea teased each other with shades of blue or the gulls that swarmed around him and waited for something to drop from his butcher block. He didn't notice our boat as it docked next to him and ten scuba divers stepped off to stretch their legs in search of a bite to eat at the Paradise Café. I was not hungry enough to drag my tired body on crutches across a long boardwalk to a restaurant that did not look open for business, so I sat and watched.

He stood with stooped shoulders under a large, royal blue, not-yet-faded, plastic and metal gazebo bolted to the new concrete dock, before a butcher-block table that looked as old as him. Long-sleeve, gray cotton shirt and pants draped his rail thin, coconut shell-colored body. His thick-soled, bleached brown leather shoes anchored him to one spot. On the table lay a mound of red snappers that looked a day beyond fresh. His whitened, crusty hands grabbed a single fish from the pile, chopped off its head then tail with greasy cleaver then pushed the remaining midsection to the opposite side of the table. After all heads and tails found their way to the scrap pile, he moved in the other direction. Without losing his steady rhythm, he slid a midsection to the center, scraped the scales with fully extended arms then pulled himself closer to slide the filet knife through the center. He wiped the filet knife after each cut with a rag that rested on the corner of the table.

I watched the man cut the fish and watched our dive master

Rinaldo move quickly about the boat as he checked, adjusted and secured tanks, ropes and gear. His strong, brown body looked restless and bored with a routine he knew well. I offered him some dry chips I discovered at the bottom of my dive bag.

"These are good. I bet you got them from the States, huh?" He asked as he munched.

"Yea." I said.

Rinaldo continued moving around the deck, in between mouthfuls of chips. The man continued to slice and the gulls continued to swarm. The Caribbean Sea slapped against the bottom of the boat. A sleepy breeze whispered through my hair.

"Where would you live if you could choose from anywhere in the world?" I asked Rinaldo.

He smiled without hesitation. "Anywhere but paradise!"

The divers returned to the boat in pairs like honeymooners concerned only with the other. Rinaldo began acting like a tour guide of Aruba again and greeted each person who stepped aboard. One man, by himself among the pairs, was my buddy on the previous dive. He was like me, traveling alone and finding dive buddies in groups of people. A real hit and miss game that I got tired of after this trip. Rinaldo started the engine of the boat and we pulled away from the dock and the man who never looked up.

My dive partner Richard and I went to dinner that evening at an outdoor restaurant. Our table overlooked the sea at sunset. A lighthouse in the distance swept its beam across the darkening horizon. The shore below us kept its own ceaseless rhythm of foamy wave against sand and rock. My freshly showered skin tingled in the warm evening breeze. Our waiter greeted us with glasses of ice water and English spoken with a Caribbean accent I couldn't imagine growing tired of hearing.

I noticed red snapper on the menu.

"Look how expensive that snapper is!" Richard commented. "Somebody is getting ripped off!"

I thought of the man cutting the fish on the dock.

"Oh well," Richard continued, "it's a financial food chain. Take before you get taken!"

"What happens if you can't move quick enough and you wind up getting taken?" I asked.

"It's a miserable place that I used to live in a long time ago and I hope to never go back there again!" Richard declared, as if he had done his time and never need look back.

I didn't explain to Richard about how I could never look at red snapper the same way again and that the hungry feeling in my stomach a moment ago had disappeared. I ordered a meal with chicken in it and sat across from Richard for the next hour as he talked about something that didn't require my full attention. While he talked, I thought of excuses I would give him later for not being able to dine or dive with him ever again.

At ten years of age, I was the second oldest of eight children. "You must be Catholic." Someone always said, whenever I told the number of siblings I had.

In our large family, I learned to share and to hide. In our large Catholic family, I learned to shut up and not question the rules, even when I wanted to scream

"Is everybody crazy?!".

"When I grow up, I'm going to buy only real milk!" My younger brother Michael declared one evening before his seven siblings, father and mother seated at the dinner table. My mother held and fed my youngest sister Tina in her arms as she tended to her other seven children. My father laughed at Michael's comment and my mother wrinkled her face in annoyance. We all knew Michael was referring to the nonfat dry milk my mother mixed in equal proportions with the whole milk she found too expensive. She never talked about it but we saw her do it every day as a way to feed her growing children and save money.

"Just wait till you have kids of your own!" she spoke with an unsatisfied vengeance.

I never knew what to say when someone commented to me about how wonderful it must be to live in such a big family or how it must never get lonely with so many people always around. I never explained that my experience in a large family consisted of exhausted, angry parents raising confused, anxious children. I wanted to believe in the fantasy about large families. Pretending something existed always felt better than living in a constant reminder that it didn't.

"Why do we go to church every Sunday?" my little brother Michael asked my mother one Sunday morning, as several of us lined up in front of the bathroom mirror to comb our hair and brush our teeth.

"Because it's a sin not to." my mother explained simply. And that was the end of that. No one could argue with sin, just as they could not argue grass was green.

We knew we had to go to church every Sunday as a family. Our reward for a tedious hour of prayer came when we went to the donut shop afterwards, where my father stood before the glass cases filled with fresh donuts and ordered two dozen from the teenage girl at the cash register.

Sometimes the man who made the donuts would perform for us behind the glass window, where he kneaded huge pillows of fluffy dough in a cloud of flour then rolled the large mass flat onto the wood table top. He amazed us with the speed of his hands as they pierced the dough with the cutter, caught the raw doughnut at its center with the opposite thumb then plopped the white ring onto the large metal frying rack. When my father walked past us with two boxes of warm doughnuts in hand, we reluctantly waved goodbye to the man we knew had the best job

Ann Kronlage

in the world.

When we got home we chose one donut each and after that it became a free for all. Sunday afternoons seemed my only chance to eat till I had enough and I ate doughnuts till my stomach hurt. The indigestion that accompanied my frantic eating did not stop me from gorging myself on doughnuts the following Sunday.

I always imagined God keeping giant score cards on every soul alive. Everybody started out with at least one mark against them, the original sin, and one's status under God depended upon the count of those deeds which we all assumed were bad or good. Lots of marks against you kept you from getting into heaven, putting you in purgatory till you could atone for your sins, or worse yet, in hell where burning was the highlighted method of suffering. Going to church every Sunday was one of those things that earned a person "good" points. God lived in the little box behind the altar, we were told as children. If we didn't visit God, he would be lonely and angry with us. It seemed holiness and fear went hand in hand; "God-fearing" was a description people who inhabited adult bodies used with pride in their voices. Fear was a state of mind reinforced at church, school, and at home.

My parents met one another when he was nineteen and she was fifteen. He was a first year college student and she was a Catholic schoolgirl. When my father graduated with an electrical engineering degree, he found a job out of state and convinced my mother to come with him and get married. Finding this to be her best opportunity to escape her poverty-stricken upbringing, my mother gave back her college scholarship and married my father.

My sister Marie came two years later. Less than two years after that, my brother Kenny arrived. Less than two years after that, I was born. Eighteen months after that, Michael was born.

Nine months later, as Joey was conceived, Kenny, at age four, was diagnosed with leukemia. Kenny died when I was three and he was four. For the last nine long months of his life, he went from home to hospital, enduring tests and medication and all the tears and fear that go with cancer or any illness that ends in physical death. Two months after Joey was born, Kenny passed away on Good Friday, 1962. At the rare times my parents spoke of Kenny, their voices became quiet, sad, slow, and heavy. The only other time their voices sounded like that was when they visited me as a patient in the burn unit.

Kenny's passing was God's will, my parents were told, and no God-fearing person could question God's will. My parents told themselves they had to be strong, to not show their fear in front of the children. Fear had become one of the great ironies of life, both encouraged and denied.

Soon Joey was baptized, at the customary age of a few months, before he even knew what fear was, to save his soul from limbo, in case he died a premature death.

Sixteen months after Joey was born, my mother gave birth to Susan. Thirteen months after that, Louis was born. Nineteen months after that, Martha was born. My mother's body began resisting delivering healthy babies, and three long years later, she managed her last one, at age 35, when my littlest sister, Tina was born.

When Tina was born, I was ten years old, and my father told me I could sneak into the hospital, under his overcoat, to see her through the nursery window. I was fascinated by my baby sister's shock of dark hair, which persistently grew straight up and out from the top of her head. When Tina came home after a few days, she also had dark hairs growing up her back. "Our little monkey." my mother joked, as she tried for over a year to get Tina's hair to lie flat on her head. Tina never smelled like a baby, but like hair spray or my father's hair cream. My mother let me hold Tina if I sat down in the easy chair, and sometimes I got to practice changing her diapers under my mother's watchful eye. "Tina is a good baby." my mother told me, explaining that Tina never fussed about anything. As an adult, I watched old home movies and noticed that Tina was a baby with large, brown, sad eyes.

By the time Tina was born, most of us understood that rules existed to teach us to obey. Children who obeyed were the best kind of children in our parents' eyes. Obedience was a sign of respect, our father continually preached. If any of us challenged the rules by not obeying them, we were disrespectful children, my father decided, and deserved to be punished. Punishment was our father's responsibility, something our mother used as a warning if we pushed her to the brink of hysteria, a point that could be heard in the pitch of her voice.

Since our father was rarely at home because of endless working days, it was usually our mother we learned to appease. Keeping her happy sometimes meant just avoiding her, or not making loud noises like arguing with each other. The same would be true when our father came home after a long day. He wanted to be alone for a little while so he sat in front of the television, ignored anyone who spoke, hit any older kid who interrupted his trance before the tube, and tolerated a younger child who crawled in his lap without a word.

As a kid at St. Martin de Porres Catholic school, I wanted to be special, exceptional, the kind of kid teachers would call on with pride. I wanted my parents to stand up tall at the sight of me and say things like, "There's nothing my little girl can't do!" or "Isn't she the most wonderful daughter in the world?" Instead, what stands out in my memory was my third grade teacher—Sister Eric Maureen—who commanded me to walk around the five rows of desks filled with my snickering peers, for an endless amount of time, for reasons I can't recall.

My sixth grade teacher, Mr. Tate, carried himself with the enthusiasm of an old bloodhound. His tired, indifferent expressions projected endless patience. I didn't consider him any other way till one day he divided our class of 11 and 12 year-olds into two math groups.

"Ann, you're in group A." He spoke with contempt.

I assumed group A to be the less prestigious of the two until I noticed the other kids in my group. I was in the same group as the smart kids! Mr. Tate seemed to resent having to put me in the smart group. What an asshole!

Somehow I missed the message for years that I was smart. Good grades in my family were considered normal, almost average. All A's on my report card usually evoked a grunt from my mother and father, at best.

My little brother Michael apparently wanted to hear from one of his parents, since he was falling behind in his grades. A kid could only stand invisibility for so long.

"I'm starting this chart today." Dad explained to the three of us; seven year-old Joey, nine year-old Michael, and ten year-old me. "If you get five checks against you within one week, you will get a spanking." He explained. We understood that checks against us came from bad things committed, like not doing homework, smarting off, fighting, or not doing our chores. I knew Michael was having the hardest time with being good, that the chart was for him more than anybody else. By the end of the week, he earned a spanking, which he got outside in the backyard under the big maple tree. It broke him of bad behavior. After that, his grades improved, he did his chores without argument, and I never heard him smart off again. He was a changed kid alright—from happy to sad, outgoing to shy, free to fearful.

Most of us were like Michael—we learned after one serious spanking what living in fear meant, that should we dare turn our backs on fear, by becoming free, fearless spirits, we would be punished, that there would be hell to pay.

Louis was one of the exceptions to those easily broken. Five years younger than me, Louis was always the bad boy, the one my parents and the rest of the neighborhood feared, and chose to blame whenever an unexplained act of vandalism occurred. Louis was the bad seed, we all knew. He seemed unimpressed by numerous spankings, which had straightened out Michael in no time. Beatings seemed to only ignite the fire inside Louis. I worried about my little brother Louis for years, sometimes certain he would eventually end up in jail, other times afraid he would grow to be a strong man, unleashing his anger upon me in the same frenzied way he fought everyone in his family. I was grateful to be bigger and stronger than him, protective toward my little sisters who seemed to bear the brunt of his cruelty, and frightened when his cries of pain and terror at the hands of my father's rage filled our house. Louis was my father's namesake, carrying on his name and his rage.

"Would you stop bothering her!" a man's voice yelled across the room, apparently at Jim, who stood before me. Jim had been shuffling the length of the ICU like Isaac. He liked to walk around the ward as if trying to get rid of the restlessness we each felt in our bodies. After I was no longer doped up on morphine, I became one of the stops on his daily walk.

"That's just Quinn yelling at me again. Don't let him scare you. He and I came in here together. We worked at the same chemical plant. There was an explosion. A beam fell on him and broke his leg and now he's in traction for six weeks, on top of the burns he got." Jim spoke with a blank expression of the horror he and Quinn survived.

Jim shuffled around the burn unit in his slippers and hospital pajamas, his left arm in a splint, making him look like a bicyclist signaling a perpetual right turn. More frightening than his painful looking burn grafts—his raw pink neck and arms dried tight like roasted turkey skin—was the bewildered and terrified look on his face.

"I just don't know what I'm going to do." he would say in his typical dazed manner.

"The best you can." I said. I wasn't about to get into a discussion with this man who seemed to want to believe the worst. It was like talking to my mother. I refused to jump on her bandwagon that all was gloom and doom.

I needed tears that had hope attached to them. I found them in a little book of Helen Steiner Rice poems that someone sent me. Sometimes I read them aloud to Jim as I cried and soon tears rolled down his face. Reading her words was both a purging and a prayer. A healthy dose of grief and praise, my friend Martin Prechtel would describe twenty five years later.

"Why is it a sin to be original?" Louis asked Sister Maura one day in front of a whole school assembly. The two hundred or so other children in uniforms seated in metal folding chairs, arranged in straight rows, became unusually quiet and still. No one laughed, which would be the usual response to serious questions directed at Sister Maura, the stern principal at St. Martin De Porres.

"Louis Bernard, why would you ask such a question?" Sister Maura yelled. "I will ask Father Scheid to answer that. Father?" She turned her red face to Father Scheid, the head priest of the school and church we all attended.

"Yes. Thank you Sister. Louis, you are confused. The original sin is not about being original, it's about a sin that we are all born with because Adam and Eve lied to God in the Garden of Eden. The sin began with the original people God created, so it's called the original sin. Understand?" Father Scheid was a better person to explain the nuances of the Catholic faith with his gentle manner, than Sister Maura with her harried expressions.

Every day someone reminded us that we were sinners first and God's children second. We were born bad and it was up to the adults around us to straighten out our thoughts and actions.

A spanking was just that, a way to straighten out our crooked ideas and behavior. If we followed the rules, God would love us more and take care of us, and so would our parents. According to Father Scheid, God had lots of rules and we were born to obey them all. The punishment for not following the rules was pain—the burning, stinging pain of Hell and my father's stick.

"Ohhhhhhh!" A long and pain-filled moan came from the men's side. It didn't sound like Jim, it was a deeper sound than he had ever produced. Maybe it was Quinn, but that didn't seem possible either, since Quinn was always so quiet.

"Who's that making that moaning noise?" I asked Jim while he paid his daily visit.

"That's Floyd." He sounded happy to be the host of the burn unit.

Floyd was not very visible like Jim. He stayed in his room, in the opposite corner from where I sat in bed. Floyd was very audible, from morning till night, and sometimes in the middle of the night. At first I felt disturbed by his deep, sorrow-filled moans. Then it was an inspiration that said to me "Go ahead and express yourself!" His moans were free where mine were always held back by fear or my own stubbornness to take the pain.

He must have been raised Baptist because he sounded like someone at a revival shouting "Amen!" The Catholic church I was brought up in never sounded like that. We were only allowed to speak at the same, predictable appointed moments and only then to repeat what the priest just said. We sat when everyone else sat, kneeled when everyone else kneeled and stood when everyone else stood. The only good thing about it all was I could daydream most of the time and no one would know the difference cause I could go through the routine in my sleep.

One day when I got out of bed, Liz encouraged me to try to push myself around the unit while she changed my sheets. I heard the familiar moan of Floyd, then saw the unfamiliar sight of Floyd. I understood, the moment I saw his burns, why he moaned all the time. His burns were only on his butt cheeks. He constantly moved from a reclining position on his bed, to standing and staring at the bed as he considered another position. His moans would come when he moved, either in or out of bed. He looked like a bear the way he lumbered his hefty light brown frame. I don't believe he meant to, but it seemed just like Floyd to moon us all—his bare buttocks with blood red saucer-shaped wounds peeked out through a skimpy hospital gown. He was definitely not Catholic.

I had never experienced such pain with anyone as I did with those men in the burn unit. Where I grew up you didn't share your pain, you swallowed it. "Offer it up." My mother would say when she knew one of us was in pain. It was her way of saying take it, but don't give it and certainly don't share it. At school it was the same thing, if I was to show fear or tears, I would be discouraged by scolding teachers or teasing classmates.

In the burn unit I watched Floyd and saw for the first time that pain did not always require suppression. A grown man could moan in agony and not be ridiculed or shamed. When I watched Floyd I hoped that someday I would be free like him.

Liz told me since I was strong enough to push myself around in the wheelchair that I was ready to use the toilet on my own. She showed me where it was and helped me with getting myself on and off it, using my arms to lift my weakened body. I was so slow, like an old lady it seemed, but I was so proud of every little thing I could do. I felt like a very patient grandmother to my tired ailing 17 year-old body.

Later, when again I made my way to the toilet that sat inside a closet like those on an airplane, I got close enough to see that someone was sitting on the toilet in the dark. It was Isaac. He didn't look up or react with a start the way I felt when I saw him unexpectedly. "I'm sorry Isaac." I said as I backed up the wheels and turned away. His reaction was so serene, so unflustered in comparison to my embarrassment. I knew in that instant that was how he had lived through all of his pain and fear. He had simply let go and surrendered to all of it. Nothing fazed him after all that he had been through. He was the epitome of fighter in the way he had overcome unbelievable odds but he didn't act like my expectation of a fighter. He wasn't angry, loud and forceful like my father acted, like I thought of if you had asked me to describe "fighter". His was strength that took a different form, strength I would find in myself in the years to come thanks to his example.

Isaac shuffled by as if unaware anyone watched him or more likely, didn't care that anyone watched him. In his thin hospital pajamas and flat slippers that gripped droopy socks, Isaac was a wisp of an old man, yet a mountain of fortitude.

"He was working as the cashier at his son's liquor store, when a desperate thief came in with a blowtorch as his hold up weapon." Liz explained with sadness when I asked her how he got into the burn unit. "Isaac sustained burns on his scalp, ears, nose, eyes, mouth, and lungs when he inhaled some of the torch flames. It is amazing to see what people survive. He's sixty-five years old and has been in here for six months. I can't remember a patient as unlikely as he was to survive and actually do it." She spoke with reverence about his determination that couldn't be seen in his scarred, hairless scalp and distorted face and ears. He never looked anyone in the eyes like he was humbled by what happened to him. The truth was we all felt humbled by him, that if we ever felt like the burn unit was too much for us to handle, we could think of Isaac and be ashamed of our self-pitying attitude. He had beat incredible odds with the one thing no one could take away from him—his will to survive.

"We're going to have to do some more debriding today." Liz and Kathy announced in the bath room one morning. When a person survives full-thickness burns, meaning the full thickness of the skin layers, there are very often small bits of flesh that have not burned away. These bits of flesh are like islands among the sea of open wounds where skin used to be. Debridement had been described to me and had been done on my body previous to that day, while I was under general anesthesia. This time I was on my own to take the pain.

After my bandages were peeled off and I was given a chance to soak in the warm water, I was told to lie down on a dry sheet-covered gurney. Liz and Kathy stood on the right side of me, each with small scissors and tweezers in gloved hands and told me it would be uncomfortable. At first I watched as Liz's long, thin hands and Kathy's large meaty hands began working together so the debriding could be finished as quick as possible. Each snip felt like digging too deeply into the side of a fingernail with clippers. A series of snips became slow torture. I looked away, held my breath and tightened my body against what felt like vultures slowly devouring me.

"How's that class going you started last week?" Liz asked Kathy calmly as she snipped my flesh away.

"I'm not sure about the instructor yet." Kathy answered as if they were talking on the phone.I thought for a split-second that maybe I could join them and forget about the pecking vultures feeling, but instead I became annoyed at their useless chatter. I wanted to tell them to shut up but I learned from my father to be careful when talking to someone who is inflicting pain on your body. Instead of speaking, I raced through, in my mind, all the words that had been spoken to me over the last few weeks.

"Offer up the pain."

"You're lucky to be alive!"

"God only gives us as much as we can handle."

"Blessed are those who suffer, for their pain will wash away their sin."

All of these voices exploded in me, having nowhere to go but out, out on the wings of my vocal cords. A roar shot out of my throat and did not stop for several minutes.

Liz and Kathy stopped for a moment. "Does it hurt?" Liz asked as if surprised. I thought for a second and realized that indeed the physical pain was barely noticeable as long as I kept yelling.

I said a quick "No." Liz and Kathy laughed nervously, then went back to pinching and snipping. "AAAAAAAAHHHHH-HHH!!!" I remember yelling as a cheerleader for hours, with enjoyment at the freedom. This time the yell was carrying me and I held on for the ride.

The hospital dietitian, Sister Mary, burst into the room and rushed over to me as if accustomed to being in charge. "Don't cry." she said simply as if comforting a child with a scraped knee. I turned my erupting head toward hers, firing my voice directly at her as if to say, "Don't tell me what to do!" Her eyes opened wide in surprise as she backed away quickly, under-standing my message. I could see Liz and Kathy smiling at the sight of me putting the self-righteous Sister Mary in her place.

I was a volcano, a spewing hot volcano of anger, frustration, aggression, disbelief and conviction that could no longer be shut off, beaten down, chewed up and spit out. Seventeen years of buildup emitted full force from my energetic lungs.

Just as quickly as I had begun, I stopped. I tried to cough the dryness out of my throat then asked Sister Mary for a lozenge. My body sunk into a hollow of relaxation as I wondered what had just happened.

"Well, now we know your lungs are in good shape." Liz joked, interrupting my thinking. The three women laughed nervously.

Soon I was dressed, helped into the wheelchair, and pushed to my bedside. My mind continued to travel, taking in all the sights and sounds around me as if for the first time. The telephone at the nurse's desk rang; the television spewed sounds of excited game show contestants, yet all of the patients and staff in the unit were quiet as my body now felt.

I looked up to see that Isaac, who before always continued past my door was instead slowly walking through my doorway. He stopped just inside and turned to apparently locate a chair that he walked toward and held onto as he pushed it toward the side of my bed. "Do you mind if I sit down for a minute?" he asked in a croaky old voice.

I nodded, stunned by his purposeful yet humble manner. He was 48 years older than me which seemed ancient but he understood what I was going through, of that I had no doubt. Just his presence fed me with the assurance that it, my life, would all turn out okay. Then he started talking very slowly with lots of breaths in between sentences.

"My great grandfather loved to tell the story of himself and a wagon full of others traveling from Alabama to wherever the road led to freedom. They were part of what was later known as the Underground Railroad." He looked me in the eyes just to make sure he had my attention. I was transfixed and he continued. "They always rode at night and had to lie down like sardines next to one another so as not to attract too much attention. The hot bumpy ride didn't bother anybody much, they had all lived through worse than that. Every stop they made was another bunch of news about what was going on, ahead of them and behind. One thing everyone knew was that when you saw a lantern hanging from a hitching post it meant that house was safe haven. It didn't guarantee no more problems just that you were one step closer to freedom. Every time he saw one of them lights it was like another hand holding him up, saying don't give up, you'll get there as long as you don't give up." He settled into the chair and smiled a little smile to himself. "I can see them lanterns glowing in the dark night. Can you see 'em yet?" he looked into my eyes.

"Yes." I said softly with tears pushing out of my eyes.

"Good." He whispered with a hoarseness in his throat. He pulled himself slowly up to standing and said "Good" again, in an encouraging kindly old way. He was finished with what he came to say. He turned and walked out the door, as slow as I had always known him.

The Smell Of Fear

Blue skies and calm waters are always a welcome sight to a scuba diver. It was one such day on Cayman Brac, when I joined a group of divers led by a dive master named Frank. I liked Frank because he knew how to take the power of the sea seriously and also had a fun-loving sense of humor. He was one of many guys I met who was born and raised in the U.S. and decided in his twenties that he wanted to explore the sea through scuba diving. Before every dive during the week I knew him, Frank educated us all with a bit of interesting information about the underwater world, in between Jimmy Buffet songs on tape he brought on board.

It was January in the Caribbean and our depth was planned at 100 feet. The water was about 80 degrees F, which can get very cold after even 5 minutes of immersion. "More attractive to sharks than blood", he announced, "is urine. So, don't pee in your wetsuit!" He turned his back and began putting on his wetsuit. We all giggled nervously, as I imagined each one of us recalled a time in the past when we were underwater and couldn't hold it any longer and made ourselves prey to the most famous predator of the sea. The shark is the master of our fear and the first thing people usually ask about when I tell them I am a scuba diver.

"Aren't you afraid you'll see one?" someone inevitably asks.

"Did you know", I say, "that you are way more likely to get hit by a car than attacked by a shark?"

It's so interesting that people fear creatures and situations outside of their everyday life more than they fear dangerous situations within their everyday life. The real danger is not necessarily out there where we are visitors. The real danger lies closer than we want to believe.

My mother recalls that for about ten years it was one of her many morning rituals to remove the fitted sheet from each of the six plastic covered mattresses of her children who were potty trained yet continued to urinate in their beds. She asked the pediatrician who told her not to be concerned, that they would grow out of it eventually. So she told herself that it was normal for six of her children to wet the bed every night for ten years.

My father ruled the house of my childhood with a shark like menace. He only had to strike once before his reputation was enough to keep most of his kids in line, like smaller fish in a school that stayed together out of fear of being eaten.

I feared my father through most of my childhood till puberty, when I became as angry as he seemed to be. I believed I hated my father and that he felt the same for me. I thought being as angry as he was made me mean as he was and that my anger could protect me.

My father visited me in the burn unit every day at dinnertime, one of the two hours of the day anyone outside the hospital was allowed into the burn unit. Every day he walked through the door, past the sign: BURN UNIT 3300, past the sign: VISITING HOURS 12PM-1PM and 6PM-7PM limited to 2 persons per patient visit. He walked past the sign warning that all persons entering must scrub hands thoroughly and wear hospital gown over street clothes, and every day he walked past the sign: NO SMOKING—OXYGEN IN USE. I waited for him every evening at six o'clock.

"Just wait till your father gets home!" My mother yelled at me in frustration, when I knew I had pushed her to the ends of her rope. "Go to your room!" she barked. I was relieved to walk away from our battle of wills. I remembered that I had been displaced from my real bed to the fold out couch in the basement, since my grandma was staying with us again and she always slept in my bed when she visited.

Downstairs was quieter and darker. My seven restless siblings were busy upstairs watching TV, doing chores, or homework at the kitchen table. In that moment, I hated them for not being in trouble too. I hated my mother for sending me to this place of fear, where all I could do was wait and listen. Listen for the garage door to open, for my father's distinguishable heavy footsteps, for the serious tones of his brief words with my mother, for the opening of the basement door, for his slower, heavier, descending manner. I would pretend I was asleep, maybe that would soften his anger, soften his hand perhaps as he swung the wooden stick or plastic brush he usually chose.

Slinking under the covers of my makeshift bed, I comforted myself by fantasizing about my father and mother, my brothers and sisters, and grandma, wailing with remorseful tears at my funeral. I floated above them all, giddy with the freedom which guaranteed no more hurt, no more disappointment.

"What (hit) do you think (hit) you're doing?" (hit) his voice warned me as his stinging blows shot me upright.

My father didn't care if I answered him, for he was somewhere else as he released his rage upon my body. I too was somewhere else, not concerned with the stinging welts rising up on my skin, rather focused on taking it, taking it and throwing it back at him with my tightening frame. I wished the pain of his contact could ricochet off me, travel back up his arm like a jolt of electricity, and into his heart. The warmth from that surge would seep in and melt his frozen core and bring him to tears, the kind of tears that say I am sorry for all of the pain I have inflicted.

As a younger child, I cried tears with a hope that he would stop. As a teenager, I told myself I wasn't going to give him the pleasure of seeing my fear.

"Your dad's here." Liz announced as she came past my door.

My dad never looked as helpless and sad as when he first walked through my door each evening. The nurses, on doctors' orders, reminded him every evening to wear a hospital gown and in the earliest weeks, a disposable mask. His discomfort with helplessness paralleled my own and in the midst of it, we attempted conversation.

My father had never shown himself to be a gifted conversationalist. When he ran out of words, he searched for cigarettes he could not smoke for the next hour, with hands that traveled nervously along the front of his body. This was a first, I thought, my comfort was put before his; he was nervous and I felt in control.

The first evening I went without morphine, he reached his arm out to touch my shoulder, and I pulled away with an exaggerated moan. I knew this would test his anger and it told me I was protected from at least the pain of him, yet it unnerved me to see him so sad.

"Everything's going to be okay." He said to me.

"How can you say that everything is going to be okay? My leg's been cut off!" I heard myself bark at him.

He lowered his face into his open hands and began to sob. If I didn't have gauze wrapped around it, my jaw would have dropped open in shock at the sight of my father crying. My heart melted with the urge to comfort him, but I told myself that somebody had to be in control.

"You'll feel better after you cry." I spoke from experience.

He looked around the room as he tried to regain his composure. "Is anybody looking?" he asked as though tears were an odd sight to behold in an intensive care unit.

"No." I said, feeling the distance grow between us.

Ann Kronlage

I recognized the dad who cried in front of me that day. I remembered him from old home movies I had watched. In one, he strolled the boardwalk of the Atlantic shore with my three year-old sister Marie and one year-old brother Kenny and he looked relaxed and happy. My mother was the one holding the camera because she was too embarrassed to be seen in front of it, since she was pregnant with me. This was the family into which I entered the world.

When my older brother Kenny was four, he was diagnosed with leukemia and nine long-suffering months later, he died in his sleep, in the hospital, on Good Friday of Easter week, 1962. My mother showed me a picture of him in the casket at his funeral. His little face was puffy from all the medication and his white suit matched his white casket. My parents saved this picture in a little white suitcase that also held a book, a toy and a sweater that was only Kenny. The suitcase has always been stored in my parents' bedroom closet, on my father's side.

There are other home movies of Kenny, Marie, and I sledding down some neighborhood hill on a bitter Boston afternoon. Kenny's cheeks were bloated and flushed red and he wore an innocent, happy smile. There were no more home movies after that for another year and a half. My sister Marie, six at the time Kenny died, recalls my father as angrier from the morning of Kenny's funeral on.

I knew him to be a kind father when he read stories to us at bedtime and recorded it so he could play it night after night on his reel to reel in our bedrooms. His gentle warm, expressive voice carried the attention of at least four of his children, whose young voices occasionally interrupted his tale with a squeal of laughter or a question.

I knew him to be a generous father when he took at least four of us on Saturdays to the "TV shop" where we knew money and ice cream awaited us. He really was an electrical engineer but layoffs spread and he joined thousands of others out of a job. He gathered together the little money available on credit and rented a small space that became Spanish Lake TV, named for the city that offered the cheapest rental property. He always loved to fix televisions, stereos, and radios for friends and family, so it seemed logical to offer sales and service as a source of income. It was a small office space in a typical strip mall of the 70's but there was an ice cream shop next door and my father was willing to pay for any job done, whether it was sweeping, dusting, polishing, paperwork, phone calls or a joke well told. My father was his own boss and on Saturdays we were the boss' personal assistants. My father was the happiest I remember when he could play inside the back of a television set with the innocence of a child beside him.

I knew him to be a kind father when I watched him fix anything with gray tape and old parts he saved around the house. I knew when he whistled through closed teeth that he was happy. I liked being his assistant, which usually meant holding something while he tightened an adjoining piece, or finding a tiny part that had fallen to a dark corner of the basement floor and watching his face widen in praise of my surprising talent.

I remembered him as a kind father when I thought of how he built a playhouse with glass windows and a real shingle roof in the backyard of our house in New Orleans. When his job as an electrical engineer transferred us all to St. Louis, he built another playhouse in that backyard with scalloped trim painted in bright circus colors. I never asked him, but I knew he still had a little kid inside him.

The little kid inside him, however, was bullied by a bigger one who set rules like children were not to smart off to their parents and if they did they got a slap. If children continued to disobey in the face of warnings, they would receive spankings.

"Like the President does to the Communists." He explained to us at the dinner table. "First sign of trouble, he sends the troops in to beat up the bad guys. We'd be just like the bad guys if we didn't fight them." I knew I would stay away from the bad guys and not disappoint my father. But then I realized there was something not right about my father's logic. He was an educated bigot driven by fear which showed up as a raging bully at home with his wife and kids. He enjoyed watching Archie Bunker but never understood people were laughing at Archie, not with him.

A bold streak ran through me as a young girl but I knew when to shut up, when to sit down, when to stop. I learned this from watching my father and guessing when he would lose his temper by the quickness of his motions, the sound of his voice, the look in his eyes.

My parents were complimented on the "difficult job it must be to raise eight kids." We each attended private Catholic school and as a family, Mass every Sunday. To those on the outside, we looked like well-tended little gardens.

Then adolescence hit me and my anger sprouted like a rebellious weed. At first, I would simply question something my father said, which would get me a slap across the face, then I would disagree with something my father said, which got me a stinging slap that left a red mark on my cheek. If I ran out of the room, he would find me and hit me more, so I told myself I would not run, but remain motionless and prove to him that I could take the pain. Once I learned to put on a stoic expression, I didn't want to take it off because I felt safer when the world couldn't see my feelings, couldn't see my weaknesses. My father tried to tease me about my growing hips, or about being afraid, or about seeing my eyes moisten when I didn't get what I wanted. Now I had the perfect weapon for all of his verbal attacks—my stone-cold face that he had helped me develop. I knew no one could ever hurt me as long as I wore that face.

My father also liked to tease my mother's mother, whether he laughed in front of her, or behind her back. My grandmother became enraged but really didn't know how to handle him except to let him lead her through an endless series of arguments. I was glad that my grandmother lived hundreds of miles away and only visited occasionally, when my mother went to the hospital to have a baby.

When I was fourteen, my mother had another baby. My grandmother settled in my room and slept in my bed, since it was the strongest frame in the house and necessary to support her obese body. Every morning, my father would say goodbye to me with a warning that if I "smarted off" to my grandmother I would get a spanking when he got home. I never lasted till the end of each of the four days, in refraining from arguing with, yelling at, or refuting something my grandmother told me. My father's spankings were really whippings, across my back, with a wooden yardstick. Each morning my father warned me, I remembered the stinging pain and his order that I sleep on my mother's side of their bed that night. I knew that I could take the pain and would smart off to my grandmother again that day, just to spite my father.

Every night, after dinner was served then taken away on a tray, after visiting hour from my father was over, bandage changing time arrived. It wasn't like a nurse came to my bed and asked if I was ready or if I had any opinion about it at all. I knew it was coming the way I knew my father would be descending the stairs after he came home from work to come find me and deliver what needed to be done. Waiting in the burn unit for what I knew from experience to be painful was very familiar to me. I had to psyche myself up twice a day—after breakfast and after dinner. I guess they chose after meals to change bandages because the experience at the very least made one lose her appetite. The waiting, the knowing what was coming as I heard them preparing the bath room, on the other side of my left wall, was so much like hearing my father's footsteps as I waited for him in the basement. I would be tough, I decided, so tough that I would impress my witnesses to the point of confusion. I could take it. What other choice did I have?

One afternoon, after lunch but hours before dinner or my father's visit, I let go and sobbed in front of Becky as she adjusted something in my room. Her usual frigid expression turned to controlled rage as she bent over my reclined body, brought her face up to mine and whispered "If you think this is bad, you should see pictures of others who never made it out of here alive!" She glared at me with a menace that stunned me. It was the look of old unresolved wounds, similar to the look in my father's eyes when he began hitting. I felt terror in that moment of knowing this out of control person had control over me.

"Would you like to see the pictures?" she threatened with an angry hiss.

"Yes." For some reason I truly was curious about others who had gone through this, no matter whether they had lived or died. She looked more furious. I felt like an animal that had just been caught in a trap and Becky was going to enjoy watching me continue to suffer. Out of my mouth came "I love you." in a soft angelic voice. I was surprised to hear myself say that, like it was not me speaking in that moment. My words surprised Becky too. She stood straight, took a few steps back, looked repulsed and confused then walked out of my room.

Later that day Becky was the nurse who would unwrap my bandages after dinner. Eddie was the other nurse, thank God. Knowing I wasn't going to give Becky the pleasure of seeing me even wince as she pulled away dried gauze that would most certainly hurt, I asked Eddie if I could hold his hand as she unwrapped me. He held out his hand and I didn't let go until it was over. About a minute into it, Eddie gave me a look as if to say "Why are you squeezing the hell out of my hand instead of letting it out the way you normally do?" I wanted to tell him what I was up to but instead I glared at Becky, held back the pain from any facial expression and continued to purge the intense stinging through to Eddie's untiring hand. He stayed right there with me in the opposite way that Becky had betrayed me earlier. As she slowly pulled at the dried gauze, she wore a smug smile as if she understood what I was doing, yet she never made eye contact with me. My determination to not flinch was fed by her controlled manner and I decided in that moment to never allow myself to be vulnerable to her again.

"There's something wrong with that nurse Becky." I told my father later. He mentioned my comment to somebody who quickly dismissed the idea that the head nurse of a burn unit who was as experienced and educated as Becky could be anything but completely appropriate and professional in all of her duties. Just like Nurse Ratched, she had them all fooled and just like Jack Nicholson's character, I would do best to stay out of her way.

The hospital psychiatrist asked me "How are you feeling about all that has happened?"

"I'm going to be just fine." I told him. He didn't understand that I was the daughter of a raging father. My stoicism impressed him and he declared me remarkably well balanced, passing out information about the fifteen minutes he spent with me like sleeping pills to all concerned, allowing them all to rest easier knowing that I would indeed endure, that my psyche could take it. I was now a certified strong courageous young woman.

In high school, I always felt comfortable with teachers who were "hard-asses", as my friends and I would call them. The driver's ed teachers were just such an example. Men in their mid to late twenties, most of them athletic coaches as well, they taught with aloof, matter of fact style. They presented the rules and the consequences of not following the rules. Mr. Burkhart and Mr. Mahon are the two I still remember. I see now, 25 years later, they reminded me of my father. I knew where I stood with them, unlike my father who passed through my day like an explosive volcano or an immature adolescent. I craved a male father figure who led the way. Those teachers became my temporary surrogate fathers. As I joined athletic teams, especially cheerleading, I traveled with them to the events and watched them as they dealt with stress unlike the way my father did. There were supportive of their young athletes; they led with a firm hand, not an abusive hand. I trusted them.

One of the most treasured cards I got in the hospital came from the baseball team coached by Mr. Burkhart and Mr. Mahon. It was a large card with a serious message about getting well. Inside, Mr. Burkhart's signature topped the list, followed by Mr. Mahon's signature, then fifty other signatures—of baseball players, basketball players, wrestlers and what looked like anyone that happened to pass the coaches in the building that day they collected signatures. I dripped a few tears on that card as I felt the strong message to keep on fighting.

Coach Burkhart went on to become a principal in the next ten years. "Coach Mahon", a friend told me years later, "was visibly distressed whenever he mentioned your name in driver's ed class. He even said one time that he felt responsible for what happened to you in a way. He felt responsible as your driving teacher because obviously no one ever told you to stay in the car if a high power line falls. He tells every class about your story and how important it is to remember."

About fifteen years after high school, I ran into Coach Mahon. He was still teaching high schoolers how to be safe behind the wheel. He didn't appear distressed as my friend described him, rather relieved to see me obviously well. His serene manner and words about God reminded me of his spiritual nature.

"There's just one thing I've always had a hard time with." I said to him.

"What's that?" He gently urged me to tell him.

"If God never gives us anything more than we can handle,

why do people commit suicide?"

He answered the question that I had been asking for years, with such wonderful fatherly wisdom. "Because they chose not to handle it."

I wanted to hug him but didn't. I couldn't explain in words all that he had done for me and from the look in his eyes, he felt the same way about me.

In high school, I signed up for endless after school activities that kept me away from my father and his anger. When I was home, I realized my father had found another child to contend with, his namesake and my youngest brother, Louis.

My father knew his job was to bring home enough money and punish any of us who weren't obedient. He never planned on what to do with children who didn't care about obedience. He never thought a child could contain a will stronger than his own. My father and mother both began to talk about Louis in front of the rest of their children as if he were a bad apple in the bunch. I began to wonder if they were right, if maybe Louis would end up in jail some day. Louis, five years younger than me, was a very angry kid, and he and I fought as much as I heard my father beat him. I was grateful to be older and bigger than Louis and tried to protect my younger siblings from his growing rage.

We knew as children, that our father owned a pistol that he kept between the mattress and the box spring of my parents' bed. I never saw him remove it from its hiding place until one day, when he casually carried it in his hand as he walked into the kitchen, checking to see if my mother, wiping a spot from the linoleum floor, had noticed him. He shot a mischievous grin at the look of terror on my mother's face, as he aimed the gun at a random spot on the wall and teased the layers of fear in her gasps and wails. He saw her as another child to be warned and I frantically prayed the gun was not loaded. I understood previous to that moment, that his gun was for protection against burglars. My father's behavior crowded out the fear of any outside menace and he became the focus of my nightmares.

"He's crazy!" my mother's scream jolted me upright in my bed. I held my breath and listened and heard only the hum of the furnace. I opened my eyes and saw only slices of moonlight on the foot of my bed. I told myself it was not real but the image of my little brother Louis being stabbed in the heart by my enraged father, as my mother, siblings and I stood by helpless, gripped me and would not let go. I jumped out of bed to go to my parents' bed. I needed to know if my father had stabbed my mother, who was seven months pregnant at the time. I stood over them as they slept for a few minutes, trying to convince myself that my father had not killed my little brother and that my mother and the unborn child she carried were safe sleeping next to him.

Soon after that, my mother delivered a premature girl who lived for thirty minutes, then passed away. It was the first time I would see my father shed a tear and I felt like a voyeur as I watched him weep for a moment then collect himself into the dad I knew.

My father lifted his head, wiped his eyes dry and sat straight up in the comfortable old chair that waited for visitors every day in the corner. He looked into my eyes.

"You're so brave. I'm sorry you're hurting." I looked at him and realized I had never heard my father apologize to anyone.

"I wish there was something I could do to help you feel better. Is there something I can do to help you feel better?" I waited a moment to let it sink in. My father was asking what he could do to help me feel better.

"Could you scratch my back? It's really been itching a lot and I can't reach it."

My back was one area of my body that had not been burned. He hesitated, said he'd be right back and returned with a washcloth in his hand. He rubbed my upper back with slow and gentle movements. I pulled away at first then relaxed with the idea that it was safe to accept comfort from my father.

Slowly, one day at a time, one hour at a time, my father and I talked to each other. He couldn't smoke cigarettes and I purposely had someone remove the television each time before he visited so that wouldn't distract him either. He told me I was brave and I listened. I told him how my day went and he listened. If I asked him to, he rubbed my back with a washcloth.

After a few weeks, he told me to decide which of my friends I would like to see and every night he would bring a different one if I wanted. I felt a little sad about the feeling that my dad was bribing my friends to visit with dinner but I pushed that worry aside for the gratitude that at least he was making an effort for me alone. Visiting hour became fun, for me, my dad and my friends.

"Do you know your dad takes whoever visits you, to dinner afterwards?" my friend Rebecca asked me one evening. "Your dad is such a nice guy." she continued. "He told me that if I felt like crying in front of you, I should, cause I'd feel better after I did."

"Really?" I said.

Between a Rock
and a Hard Place

CHAPTER 6

From out of the window of a descending plane, the Caribbean waters that meet island shoreline never look one color, rather a series of blue then green rings that announce the changing depth. Bonaire was the island this time. One of the ABC islands (Aruba, Bonaire and Curacao) off the coast of Venezuela. "DIVER'S PARADISE" said the brochure. For the seven short days I spent on the island of Bonaire, it became a paradise of more than just diving.

At the age of 35, I had not dated a man who lived within my time zone for several years. The men I attracted were those I met while on diving vacations. I became a different woman on vacation compared to home. After a few hours of guilt about being away from my children, I glowed with gratitude toward everyone and everything around me.

There were no manufactured tunnels that kissed the exit doors of the plane and hurried us out into a terminal that bustled with people. Instead, the exit doors led immediately down a metal open staircase, into the warm, moist, salty air. A man with dark brown skin greeted us with a warm smile then directed us to proceed to the customs counter. Two men at customs stopped their friendly conversation and walked slowly behind opposite counters, where we waited in line for them to first ask for a passport which they stamped with proof of our entry.

The twelve of us climbed into two taxi vans waiting for us after being told our luggage would arrive on the next incoming flight, approximately two hours later. Some of us groaned, but most of us realized we didn't need our luggage right away and were happy to just be off the plane.

I traveled with a group of divers I barely knew. A friend once asked me why I kept taking vacations with strangers. I had to explain that my vacations were for doing something different, something I could never do at home. I didn't know anybody in my immediate circle of friends willing to dive and spend the money to do it in the Caribbean. My hunger for adventure was too great to wait for someone I already knew to join me. I decided as long as one of my siblings agreed to stay with Willie and Annie while I was gone for a week, nothing would hold me back.

Five minutes out of the airport, we arrived at Captain Don's Habitat, a complex of two-story hotel units and individual cottages. Our group had reserved cottages that accommodated two to four people each. After walking to my cottage that had four beds and meeting my roommates, I knew I needed to be alone after a long day of constant people and constant noise.

I strolled along the concrete walkway that gently curved in between and around the other cottages, toward the sound of a live calypso band. A man and woman sat together at a tiny thatch-decorated bar next to where the band played. The bartender talked to them between glances at the television. It was set to a cable news station from the U.S. where a constant flow of sports and politics could be counted on. The band and bar sat on a raised piece of land that overlooked the Caribbean Sea. In between songs, the sounds of the gentle surf welcomed me. I walked away from the noise of people and their familiar sounds, into the soft, quiet night.

I continued on the softly lit walkway toward what someone told me was a restaurant. Relaxed footsteps and gentle words could be heard as I decided to greet every pair of eyes that met mine along the way.

Ann Kronlage

"Hello." I greeted a man about my age walking toward me. He had a stern expression on his face that didn't change as he replied "Good evening." He held his gaze on my face till we passed one another. How could a person appear so tense in a place of such spacious beauty? I wondered.

I saw him again the next morning among many divers washing their gear in a giant steel tub of water. He was wearing a tiny nylon bathing suit and walked carefully across the boardwalk to the lockers where each diver could store cleaned gear. He had a perfectly sculpted body, so perfect I laughed to myself at the sight of him. He looked like one of those muscle men trying to win a trophy for best body competition.

"Do you dive alone?" The Mr. World contestant asked me the next day as I fumbled through my own gear in search of fin and snorkel mask. I understood him to be asking me if I was with a male partner on this dive vacation, but was surprised by his way of asking. Sweet nonetheless, and I was a sucker for sweet. I answered yes to his question. He seemed so different from the arrogant and uncaring man I noticed earlier.

Then he asked me to help him take off his wetsuit at the shoulders—a normal request after a just completed dive. Again I got a sense of arrogance when he stood like a peacock initiating a mating dance. He lost my interest in that instant and I walked away with my dry gear in hand, toward the edge of the pier.

I sat on the edge, dangling only my whole leg over since doing so with the other leg often loosened my prosthesis off as a shoe slips off a relaxed foot. The clear water five feet below me sparkled with a hint of green. I decided I would snorkel with my clothes on, close to the pier, just to acquaint myself with this intriguing environment.

"Do you night dive?" I heard his voice say above me. He had followed me and wore his sweet and humble mask again.

"No." I answered without hesitation while the nightmare of my last and only night dive experience raced through my thoughts. "It is too dangerous. The last time I went diving I had the world's worst buddy and instructor. I don't want to go night diving ever again." I blurted out my fear and noticed his calm face take on a look of misunderstanding.

"You must speak slowly. I am a new student of English. My name is Gunther. I am from Hamburg. You are from the United States, yes?" He held out his hand and gave me a warm handshake.

"Yes. My name is Ann." I felt more curious about this person who came from a place I had never been.

"Are you afraid, with night diving?" He asked, like a small child who understood my hesitation.

"Yes." I admitted.

"You must not be afraid. I will not let anything bad happen to you." His words fell out of his mouth so gently and sincerely that I knew I could not refuse his offer to join me at sunset for a night dive along the shore where he had been the last two nights with another diver.

"I only wear one fin because I have an artificial leg." I spoke while glancing down at my legs. I gave him a chance to back out in case he wasn't ready for a woman with an amputated leg. I became anxious with the feeling of attraction I felt for this man.

For the next six days we communicated as if always under-water—with few words and a fascination toward viewing another from a very different world.

Four hours later, we met at the same pier. The sun, a reddish ball of fire, surrendered to the cool of night as the calypso band serenaded our descent.

It had been a year since I went scuba diving at night. I had told myself it was the instructor or my buddy that night who

Ann Kronlage

were to blame for my horrible experience. By the time I reached ten feet of depth I knew it was my own inexperience that deserved the blame. I didn't understand the importance of neutral buoyancy on my first night dive, but I did experience the importance of it on my second night dive with Gunther. Not maintaining neutral buoyancy on a night dive is like walking across a room while an earthquake is happening beneath your feet. Maintaining neutral buoyancy on a night dive is like floating effortlessly across the same room without disturbing anything in your path. I had experienced the former on my first night dive and the latter that night I met Gunther.

We began our dive by following the rocky edge just beneath the surface of the salty, warm, clear water, combing the large, black boulders with our flashlights. He spotted it first, an octopus! Watching it as it moved along the uneven landscape, we witnessed the kaleidoscopic talents of this amazing creature. It changed so many times within a few minutes I wasn't sure whether it did so in response to its variegated background, or its mesmerized audience. As it changed colors, hues, and combinations, it also changed shape, reminding me of a half-set glob of animated gelatin. We didn't fear its infamous spray of ink, and perhaps it didn't fear us enough to use that weapon. Instead, we drifted effortlessly along, our eyes glued to this incredible, ever-changing sight, seizing the opportunity given to us. It was inevitable that our new acquaintance would disappear into the hard surface it knew as home, heightening my excitement further. We touched its squishy covering with our carefully placed fingertips, hastening its departure. For a fleeting moment, I prayed it would stay within our sight, and just as quickly it shrank into a crevice in the rock. A wave of gratitude and disappointment washed over me as I continued staring for a minute, hoping for an encore performance.

I didn't realize then that I had stumbled upon a fitting metaphor for my mother. She is the octopus, it seems, the parallel of having eight limbs (children) just the beginning of the similarities between the two of them. Her ever-changing facade has always kept me wondering, alert to the mystery that is mother, confused as to whether she made decisions to conform to the inflexibility of those around her, or in an attempt to elude those who reached out to her.

As a teenager in the hospital, I was again disappointed, for, like the octopus, my mother was still slipping away and changing colors, keeping me at a safe distance.

She entered my room every day with a terrified look on her face, as if she argued with her feet to stay and to continue walking forward into this chamber of pain. There has always been an unspoken agreement of silence in our family. "Offer up the pain." Or don't talk about it and eventually the pain will go away. She didn't ask me to offer up anything and we both avoided talking about the pain that surrounded us like a surging sea.

I waited for her, every day, helpless in my own urge to run from this place which I had awoken to; praying each day that she would not disappear behind her tears again.

Her sodden eyes seemed unable to see anything but futility in my pain. The only emotion she could summon before me was her fears, her tears, as she shrunk into an amorphous glob of sadness.

What a cruel coincidence it was that fourteen years earlier, on Easter Sunday, she and my father buried Kenny at the age of four, after nine months of battling leukemia. Her pain was so great, she tried to bury it beneath endless hours of hard work as a mother. Staying busy was easy to do, and kept the pain at a distance.

Fate had delivered another stinging blow to her now, as another child sat before her, gravely ill, on the anniversary of the death of her big brother. My mother's terror could no longer be buried, rather exhumed, and she was forced to relive her painful past every time she looked at me.

Ann Kronlage

One morning I was brought into the bath room for bandage changing and told "A group of medical students will be coming through this morning to observe you without your bandages. Do you mind?" I felt excited at the idea of being an object of interest to strangers as I reclined on my back in the tub and wet towels were draped over my hips and breasts. All my bandages had been removed and my right arm was chosen as the favored specimen for the visitors soon to arrive. Bloodied raw hamburger is how I would have described the surface of my right arm. I was getting used to seeing it twice a day. Apparently not everybody had the same experience I did.

"Don't be upset if, when they come through", Liz said, "one of them feels faint and has to leave the room." I know her words were meant in kindness but the truth of them slapped me in the face at that moment. I was not a subject of interest so much as a site to be endured by students studying medicine. Fortunately, when they did enter the room, they came in behind me, observed my raised arm as a voice told them a little bit of my history of injuries and we never saw each other face to face. No one fainted or had to leave the room unexpectedly, before they quietly herded themselves out.

I remember many times growing up, when my mother stood fully clothed before the full-length mirror in my parents' bedroom. "Look at that fat butt!" she chastised her body. She did so before at least two of her children, and often her husband, fishing for compliments, but usually getting a condescending assurance from my father that she was indeed as ridiculously unappealing as she had feared. At a time in my life when I hung on my parents' every word, this exchange between them affirmed to me that a woman's worth lay in her physical features. It told me that a woman's place was not in the kitchen so much as it was in the endless pursuit of approval by standards and persons beyond her control. I believed the message for a few years, learning to be obsessive about the sizes of my body parts;

regarding my thick toes, my wide fingers and hands, and my large jaw and skull as shameful characteristics which I would be burdened with for the rest of my life. It was only after I lost most of my toes, and nearly some of my fingers, that I realized how foolish we all were, how much of a lie we were all living.

It was a running joke in my family growing up, among the females, headed by my mother, that we had very unattractive toes and feet. We had wide feet with wide toes and toenails. We agreed our toes and feet looked like men's feet, in fact the best fitting shoes for comfort were men's shoes. When I was around ten or so I remember loving the summer rains that fell in Missouri. The clouds would dump their moisture for at least an hour, making the street curbs into rivers and inviting me to wade along their edges. After I got my fill of immersing my feet in the warm summer rain I went to our backyard where a familiar plot of earth had transformed to mud after the healthy rain.

It was never disputed by anyone I knew of that our feet and toes were ugly. Never disputed in my mind until I woke up in the ICU and saw what was left of what I considered ugly. Out of ten toes I was born with, I had one remaining—the big toe on my right foot, and even that one had no toenail. A missing toenail was not an important loss compared to the rest of my body so I never asked and no one ever brought it up. The second and third toes on my right foot were just a third of their original length. Just nubs with tender bony ends that I would later discover hurt like hell when I stubbed them. The funny thing about these funny toes of mine is that I could no longer dare refer to them as ugly. They were there which made them beautiful. They survived with the rest of me which made them noble, amazing and worthy of only tender loving care. The struggle down the road would be remembering to cherish a body that a large majority of the society regarded as mutilated.

The sight of my body would bring men to their knees, but not for what we know as yearning. It would make them weep, but not for what we know as longing. It would leave them speechless, but not for what we know as desire. That was the message I got from my mother and from the culture that raised her and I and everyone I knew.

With one step out of the car I had become a living manifestation of all that my mother feared: death, pain, being horribly different and therefore unacceptable to others. She never spoke to me about how she felt, since words required an understanding of feelings and we were both barely keeping our heads above the water in an ocean of feelings. She entered my room everyday in tears and said goodbye in tears. I saw her daily visits as joyous opportunities to finally reach her, as it had been with my father, but she found reason to slip away each time. Again I had the feeling that I treaded water out from a shore where my mother and others in my life stood watching, terrified for me and yelling that they couldn't rescue me because they didn't know how to swim. I knew without anyone telling me that if any rescue was going to happen it had to be up to me. I would discover in the years to come that being surrounded by a world that says you have to do it yourself is both an alienating and liberating feeling.

I changed my focus from her to someone else one day, her mother. "Tell me about Grandma when you were growing up." I said.

Her face softened with relief as she thought about her mother. "My mother? I feel as though I have never known my mother. Like she never let me get close to her. Let's see.... My parents were both uneducated and lazy people. My father adored my mother, and he adored me, but he really was a simple-minded man. He thought cutting grass was the best he could do to earn a living, while my mother worried that the neighbors would find out that we were desperately poor. Ha! Imagine her thinking that anybody didn't already know! She kidded herself about everything. She couldn't see that she was fat, dirty, and lazy, and

I'm afraid she still is. By the time I left my parents and brother behind, and married your father, I knew I never wanted to be anything like my mother. And that is the best thing I can say about her." My mother looked away with a sigh, as though shy to admit such things to me.

I had always sensed my mother's opposition to Grandma. I understood why she prided herself on staying slim, clean, and well dressed. In contrast to her mother, she was active and busy, with seemingly boundless energy. My mother, who bore ten children with her body, left her own mother in the dust, complaining of the physical endurance of having two. Her mother married an uneducated man, while she married a college graduate with a promising future ahead of him. Her mother, who had become hard with bitterness, married a placid-tempered man, while she, still soft with submissive enthusiasm, married a man who eventually showed a raging temper.

It seems she had reached her goal in life—to be nothing like her mother. As she found herself immersed in all that was not her mother's, I reached out to her in all the ways that a daughter does.

I reached out to her with rebellion, and she slipped away from me with "Wait till your father gets home!" I reached out to her by emulating her; she slipped away with criticism of the way I did it. She changed colors by saying "Don't argue with me!" as I developed, then later inquired "Why can't you think for yourself?" She changed colors by saying, "Don't hit your little brothers and sisters.", while she turned a deaf ear and a blind eye to her husband when he did the same to her young children. I reached out to her with good grades, she slipped away by saying "Those are just public school E's, they don't mean the same thing as Catholic school E's." She changed colors by having eight kids, but never seemed to enjoy the company of children. I reached out to her by doing what I thought she would approve of and she slipped away by finding only fault in what I did.

Ann Kronlage

When I reached adolescence, I scorned her and knew I didn't want to be anything like her. When I reached the burn unit, I waited every day like an infant for my mother to tell me she had the answers for me—that she knew what I needed to make all the pain go away. I imagined that because she was my mother she would be able to dig deep somewhere in her soul and tell me the wise thing to do. What am I going to do with my life now that this has happened to me? My eyes bored into her every day.

"If only we had sent you to a different high school, then this never would have happened." My mother said many times when she visited.

"Mom, you've always said, 'If if were a skiff we could all take a boat ride.' Don't you remember that?" My mother looked at me in a fog of confusion.

"If only I had said no when you asked to use the car that night. If only Rebecca had not been with you that night, then this never would have happened. Goddamnit! Why did this have to happen?" She threw her face into her hands and sobbed some more. I cried at the sight of her crying. I cried because she didn't know what to do. I cried because no one knew what to do. I cried for the sadness of it all. I cried for the young woman I was who still didn't have her mother there as a source of strength, only an example of fear. I cried for the young woman who still tried to reach her mother.

"Ellen Kaiser asked about you the other day when I saw her at church. She wanted to know if you had a lot of pain." My mother said.

"What did you tell her?" I asked, interested that someone like Mrs. Kaiser thought of me.

"I told her yes, that you had a lot of pain." My mother said with pride in her voice. I knew she wouldn't have that kind of conversation with just anybody but Ellen Kaiser was different.

Ellen had slipped in and out of any sort of social contact at church since being told she had cancer. Ellen was my mother's age, had three kids and a husband and cancer that was consuming her. Rumor was that she went to Mexico to find a treatment that the U.S. couldn't provide. To share news of my pain with her through my mother felt oddly comforting. I like to think that it helped her as much as me to hear that someone else understood daily, continuous pain.

As an adult I asked my mother why it was she never wanted to get very close to me. "With so many kids, it was all I could do to provide for your physical needs. I didn't have any idea there was something beyond that. There were times when I fantasized about leaving your father, but then what could I do to take care of myself? And how could that help you kids if I left? I told myself to feel grateful if my children were at least doing well in school and that we all had enough money to get by. There simply wasn't enough time to think about anything more."

She raised her children in an atmosphere of confusion, led by her fears, the way the octopus navigated itself in an atmosphere of confusion, of constant changing colors, led by its fear that something would get too close. Both of them would inevitably find themselves stuck between a rock and a hard place.

She changed colors like the octopus, doing so to blend in with the world around her. "In those days, a wife always tried to do the agreeable thing, to keep the peace at whatever cost, between her and her husband. He always criticized me, though, having me believe I was stupid, worthless, and crazy. And I believed him. So I stuck around also to find out what was wrong with me." My mother confessed to me years later, after she found the financial and emotional independence to live on her own, away from my father.

Lunch arrived in the burn unit about the same time my

mother did every day. The food was good for hospital food, but I rarely had an appetite. Less than a month earlier, when I was an energetic, active, but overweight teenager, my mother begged me to stop eating. In the hospital, my mother joined the rest of the staff in begging me to eat. She changed colors to suit her surroundings again; first because society told her I should be eating less, then because the professionals told her I should be eating more. Why is it we could easily talk about how much I should eat, but be clueless as to what other nourishment I needed?

She urged me to eat, to swallow what was being offered to me, when all I was able to do was regurgitate. My body seemed to be rejecting, with its nausea, what my heart could not articulate in its sadness, what my soul could not express in its despair at finding loneliness in everyone and everything.

Her advice to me as a woman was to take what life had to offer and swallow it. What she didn't understand was that while a person is busy swallowing, her body is physically incapable of speaking, of asking why? Keep swallowing, my mother told me. I can't keep swallowing, Mother.

My vomit is the seeping fluid of my damaged tissue, the tears I shed, the sweat I excrete as I struggle inside to explain it to you. You are sitting before me mother, upset that my vomit has made such a mess, yet I am sighing with relief that the painful pressure in my gut has finally subsided. Amongst all of this horror there is joy, for it is the voice of my soul—and it has miraculously, finally been heard.

My mother stood before me, fixated on my physical nourishment, but what of my emotional and spiritual nourishment? Of the latter, I have always felt malnourished, and the pain of hunger I feel is no longer in my stomach, but in my heart and in my soul. There was an urgent cry from within me that I could no longer ignore, and I was reaching out to her with my bandaged arms, my aching heart, and my determined soul.

For two weeks after the doctors and nurses cut off my left foot, I laid unconscious from continuous injections of morphine that I was allowed to request every two hours. During that same time the doctors and nurses warned my mother and father of the danger of possible further amputation, this time of my left hand which lay cold at my side from lack of circulation. My mother described to me years later how she sat beside me those few days and held my stiff, cold fingers in hers, tenderly rubbing and praying for the blood and warmth to return to the tips of my hand. It was one of those rare moments when she was not slipping away from me. My body, although deep in its unconscious state, could sense that she was finally reaching out. Every cell of my being leapt out to her in ecstasy, flowing freely in anticipation of contact. She held tight, until I awoke, and the doctors announced that an amazing recovery had occurred, that amputation was no longer necessary.

Do you remember telling me about how the doctors expected me to go into a feverish delirium like all other burn patients had? And that miraculously I never did? And that I had started my period with Becky standing over me saying that was impossible? What does that say to you Mother? What it says to me is you can't believe something just because somebody says it's so. Like my life is over for all useful purposes, the way your eyes tell me you believe. Believe in possibilities, not in your fears.

Keep holding tight, Mother. Don't be dictated by your fears by slipping away or changing colors. Instead of waiting for conditions outside of yourself to change, decide unconditionally. Instead of being led by fear, be led by love, unconditional love. That's what I need from you Mother, more than anything else —unconditional love—nothing more, nothing less.

I appeared so calm to you, so unbelievably strong, yet what has given me this strength is unconditional love I have found for myself. This is what the psychiatrist saw in his assessment of me and this is what the doctors and nurses call an amazing

99

recovery—unconditional love. This is my faith in God and this is what makes me a survivor—unmistakable, unconditional love. That is what you found in yourself as you rubbed my left hand back to life.

You cannot touch nor comfort my body, Mother, but you can touch and comfort my soul—by swaddling it with your unconditional love. By letting your tears wash away your fear, and see your daughter with a newborn vision which loves purely, selflessly, unconditionally. When you see me with unconditional love, you will see my life as not ending, but rather just beginning.

I will be the voice for you Mother. The voice that speaks with words and actions that demonstrates how you and I, how everyone in our culture has been duped. The voice that speaks with a body scarred, dismembered, and shaken but not finished. Thrust into adulthood, you said about my life now. Let's walk together then. Hold each other up. Ready?

Seeing The Light

"There's a fish out there who loves to tag along with the night divers. We call him Charlie because he looks like a tuna. Don't be nervous if you see him. He's harmless." The dive manager at Captain Don's Habitat resort said to a group of divers, of whom I was one.

It was the morning after we stepped off the plane, after we were told our luggage was a flight behind us, after we had enjoyed a delicious breakfast outside on the raised rocky shore, right where we now sat to hear our orientation talk about diving in the marine park reserve surrounding Bonaire. Scuba diving could be done from the pier twenty-four hours a day, but a few ground rules had to be established, he explained. I didn't wonder about Charlie for too long because I had decided I would not be night diving.

That is until I met Gunther later that day and he charmed me into trying night diving with him. For the next five nights and days I was captivated—by the water, by the land, by the creatures and by him. It was wonderfully unhurried to have the option to jump off the pier whenever one felt like it, instead of the usual routine of climbing on a crowded boat that drove for as long as 30 minutes to get to a site. For me it was more like a slipping into the water because I always removed my prosthesis before. Gunther and I descended each evening before the light of the day left the sky, into the shallow, shadowy sea, where on the first night I discovered neutral buoyancy. Reading about it in a book or being told about it was like all of diving—before you actually experience it you will never fully comprehend it. It clicked inside of me the way motherhood clicked. I had learned in the Bahamas that I needed only 4 pounds of weight on my belt instead of eight that everybody gave me. Four pounds made all the difference.

We swam toward the right, in search of a wall that the dive manager described as a continental shelf. The wall stretched for miles, he said, and was a good guidepost to use for night diving. If we watched both time and air in our tanks, turning around at the halfway point would make for an easy dive. The wall beside us would be teeming with night creatures, he assured us in the morning orientation.

We swam along the wall in a direction that was against the current so our return would be with the current. Gunther settled in at 60 feet of depth while I hovered above at 40 feet. I was grateful to have a powerful fin. Wearing just one, I was able to keep up with Gunther's steady pace. We scanned the wall to our right with our flashlights, anxious for any movement of color or shape. Within a few minutes, I sensed a creature on the left side of me. I looked down at Gunther to see he hadn't noticed what had come beside me. I turned my head slowly to the left as I continued kicking my single fin. I didn't look face to face with it as that, I decided, could provoke an attack. It was less than an arm's length away from me! In full scuba gear, including a wetsuit, it's hard to turn quickly anyway, but I knew a panicked reaction would just encourage the same from the swimming creature next to me. There was nothing I could do but remain calm, I reasoned with my accelerating heartbeat and breath. I turned to the right again, surveying the wall with my flashlight.

Suddenly a shiny chrome panel darted out in front of my light and stopped at the wall. It was the creature that had been swimming next to me! Within the time it took to read this sentence, it returned to my left side. This huge fish, which I estimated to be about as long as me, was looking for food. This was

Charlie that the dive manager had talked about that morning! He had the shiny, silver coloring of a tuna, but he was actually a tarpon. It was obvious he liked the night divers because their flashlights helped him find food. I must have missed that part of the dive manager's talk.

Charlie stayed by my side for the rest of the dive, interrupted about every five minutes by a food sighting, when he repeated the flash, dash and return trick. He's just a big, friendly fish, I concluded, unless you're a small fish under his watchful eye. For the next six nights, he joined Gunther and I on our night dives along the same wall, usually staying at my side. I assumed he preferred the 40-foot depth I stayed at and by the end of the week he became my second dive buddy.

Gunther and I were inseparable for the next five days, except for the first two nights of fitful sleep, when I heard his German-accented English whisper as if he were there beside me. Our conversations above water were as wordless at times as below the surface. He was just beginning to learn English because he wanted to be a pilot and certified pilots had to communicate in English he explained to me. We both agreed that more than just the small amount of words were being communicated. He felt more understood than ever and I felt special in the arms of a man so attractive, so wealthy, so exotic and so ready for adventure. We looked so much alike, with strong square jaws and dark hair and eyes, as though even our bodies recognized one another. Six weeks after we said goodbye in the Caribbean, he flew to me in the U.S. The tension between us grew as we realized this love affair would not last. I gave it one last try when I went to him in Hamburg. We parted the last time in searing anger toward each other.

All of the significant relationships in my life had been with angry men. It made sense if you believed like attracts like. Anger became the fuel behind my life force when I reached adolescence. Anger kept me fighting in the burn unit. I assumed

God's anger fueled the force of the electricity and my subsequent injuries and pain. Why was God so angry with me? Every morning I silently asked that question of Him. I fantasized that because I struggled so deeply every day with something that everyone agreed was horrifying, that I would be rewarded with a magnificent explanation from God. I know now that God answers prayers in subtle ways, with thoughts and feelings that gently penetrate our beings.

Every afternoon in the burn unit, after my mother left and after the lunch trays were taken away, the hospital priest walked into my room. He held a chalice filled with Communion hosts in front of him as if it were a shield. He was obviously uncomfortable with either me or the Burn Unit, I knew that from the first day I met him. If this man of the church could not even tolerate being in this place which I had no choice but to tolerate what did that say for the institution he represented, the institution that purported all my life to be the liaison to God?

His routine was like the dry procedure of all the Catholic masses I had ever attended. He said hello, asked me if I wanted Communion that day, stepped a little closer if I said yes, spoke a short prayer as he picked up a single wafer in his thumb and index finger then moved it toward my obedient outstretched tongue. If I said no to Communion he kept his distance. I only got a short prayer and sign of the cross aimed in my direction, then a quick getaway with the excuse of many people to see. On days I told him yes, he looked pleased to get the chance to perform his entire routine for me.

He looked as old as my grandfather and in the first few days I imagined he would have some wonderful words of wisdom to pass on to me. It soon became obvious that the only thing this puppet of the Catholic Church had to offer me was the small bit of blessed unleavened bread. I played his game like a puppet also, by closing my eyes, sticking out my tongue and swallowing what he gave me.

One day, with my father at dinner time, in walked Father Muesenfechter. He was the head priest at St. Martin de Porres and had earned the title of Monsignor, the significance of which I never understood. Here was a man of God who could give out advice, I thought, as he first entered my room. After a few words of greeting came out of his mouth, however, it was obvious he could only relate to me as he had in church—from a distance with a rehearsed litany of words. It would begin the dethroning of the Catholic church in my heart and soul.

"Father Zisker has offered to come visit you. Would you like that Gussie?" My mother asked me one day. Father Zisker was the cousin of a family we knew for years, in the neighborhood and in church. He was a recently ordained priest, a man just a few years older than me and I hoped he could help me more than the old puppet.

"Hello Ann, I'm Father Zisker." He spoke gently. I couldn't sit up that day so he sat in a chair on the side of my bed. He brought me a gift. A beautiful cross made of roughly whittled wood hanging from a leather thong. "It was made by monks in Central America." He said reverently as he attached it to the top of the IV pole next to the bed.

"Thank you." I said, admiring it.

"It will protect you in here." He said with a soft smile as he sat down again. My thoughts lingered in the silence as we both wondered what to say next. "Would you like me to hear your confession?" He asked. I agreed, grateful that he didn't offer me Communion.

As I listed my sins, I wished I could admit to something truly immoral in my past. It would mean I could get it out, have it absolved and bring a logical conclusion to God's wrath as I saw it. I wallowed too deep in shock to be able to ask the question "Why?" aloud. A tear fell from Father Zisker's eye as he listened. I think he understood my confusion. I will always be grateful for that. He did the best that anyone could have done for me then. He simply listened to me as I talked.

Fifteen years later, I sat next to Father Zisker at a Cub Scout meeting.

"Do you remember me? You came to visit me in the hospital." I said gently.

"Why yes!" He looked relieved and a bit surprised as we shook hands. I heard he left the priesthood several years earlier and married a woman who left the convent. They had three kids, one of which belonged to the same Cub Scout troop as my son Will. There was silence again between us but this time it was a good silence. We looked at one another for a moment, proud of how far we both had come.

"There's a new patient coming into the burn unit in a few minutes. I have to get him settled in." Kathy said after she had come to my bed to see why I pushed the buzzer. I convinced her to get the wheelchair for me without telling her I was curious to see this new patient. I pushed myself out to the men's side of the unit, in front of Jim's, Quinn's and Isaac's beds.

Floyd stepped out of his room and stood at the nurses' desk. He didn't say anything, looked at the phone that someone was using then turned and walked back into his room. I guessed he was waiting to use the phone. I pushed my wheelchair over to the nurses' desk, thinking more information about this new patient was more likely had from one of the staff. I waited with alert eyes and ears as everyone around me moved, talked and carried things in preparation for the new arrival. Floyd stood next to his bed and spoke to me.

"Hey Ann, can you tell me when that phone's available?" he asked.

"Sure Floyd." I said, feeling privileged to be useful to someone for a change.

After a few minutes someone gave me the phone so I could reach it and I looked at Floyd who walked a few steps toward me. "Can you dial the number I give you?" he asked with a smile like he was up to something. I was ready for anything fun so I started dialing. "Ask for Shirley." He said after I told him it was ringing. A woman answered the phone and I asked for Shirley.

"Who is this?" She asked very suspiciously and Floyd's face lit up with a big smile as he held his hand out to take the phone from me. I gave it to him and he started talking. "Don't be jealous baby that's just a patient here in the hospital with me." He teased her with a big grin on his face at me. I felt so grown up being his partner in crime and being able to make a grown woman jealous. It had been a while since I had that much fun.

"Hey Ann, did you hear we're getting another patient in here?" Jim asked me.

"Yeah, I wonder how badly he is hurt." I spoke with a perverse hope it would be as bad as me.

"I heard it is a man who turned his dune buggy over and got burned when it caught on fire." Jim said as if excited to be the first one to tell me.

"That doesn't sound very interesting." I said, feeling disappointed.

Our new patient's name was Bruce and he had been injured just as Jim said. He was about twenty-five with reddish hair. He didn't talk much except for one time when he yelled from his bed for someone to change the channel on the television. I was rolling happily nearby in my wheelchair in order to get some strength back in my left hand. "I'll do it!" I said excitedly as I made my way to the television. The expression on Bruce's face told me he felt ashamed for having less initiative than a pathetic amputee like me. He jumped up and beat me to the TV. "I'm sorry, I'll get it." He said without looking in my eyes. I had a sinking feeling of despair that he didn't believe I could accomplish such a small task.

The last patient I saw come into the burn unit was younger than me. Fourteen year old Ricky had been siphoning gasoline from something when it exploded in his face. His burns were mostly on his face. When it was his turn to get his bandages changed, he screamed "I can't take this!" so loud and so many times, I wanted to yell back through the wall at him "Stop being such a wimp!" I never did talk to him though and wonder still why I had so little empathy for him or Bruce.

"When you see your grafts take, you will feel so much better." Eddie and Liz said as they changed my bandages after dinner. I wondered what it would feel like to be excited about something in my life and hoped they were right.

The first graft operation I would remember took place in less than a week and everyone prepared me for it. They talked to me about how I couldn't eat for twelve hours before going into the operating room. They talked to me about what would happen in the operating room, how the doctors would remove skin from parts of my body that weren't burned, like my abdomen and right leg, and graft it to the parts that needed it. They said the best donor skin was from the patient herself and that tissue rejection was least likely in that situation. I was lucky to have only 40% of my skin burned because that meant a lot of choices for donor skin. I was lucky to be so young they kept telling me. They also explained that after surgery, I would have to lie completely still for a solid week and if I couldn't it would reduce the chances of the grafts taking. I imagined the grafts to be like sod placed in a bare spot on the lawn. The less anyone disturbed it, the better the chances it would root and fill in the dead spots.

"That's right!" Liz sounded so excited that I understood that I hated to argue the fact that I wasn't stupid. It was easier to play the helpless patient role because it seemed to please her more and I had learned pleasing people got you more than arguing with them ever did.

When the day of surgery arrived, I could only smell

breakfast come through the burn unit. When lunch came, I covered my ears with a pillow so I wouldn't hear the sounds of people enjoying their food. By the time dinner arrived, I felt so hungry I asked about surgery.

"The burn patients are always last in the day's schedule so that the operating room can be sanitized thoroughly before the grafting takes place. There is so much opportunity for infection, we have to be extra careful." Kathy explained it so that I couldn't complain about my empty stomach. I was so hungry I felt too dizzy to even sit up.

I awoke in the recovery room, immediately aware of the sharp stinging pain on my abdomen and lower right leg where skin had been removed for grafting. It was the same skinned knee stinging that I felt when my bandages were peeled off, yet this pain could not be soothed by a soak in the tub. I felt an urge to move so as to somehow relieve the pain, but the man in hospital scrubs and mask next to my bed told me I was not to move at all if I wanted the grafting to be successful. I liked the way he spoke so gently that I didn't mind doing as he suggested. He told me he was there to monitor me as I came out of anesthesia and that I would return to the burn unit in a little while.

I stayed awake as he pushed me slowly and quietly down several hallways and on one elevator. Noises and lights were the harshest on my ears and eyes each time I woke from surgery, which made me more grateful for my soft-spoken escort and the dark lights of the late night burn unit as he pushed me beside my new bed.

I was lifted from the bed by Doris, Liz, Eddie and the soft-spoken man from recovery, and placed onto a circular frame bed. Someone told me I would have this temporary bed for a week so I wouldn't have to move. It was a bed that could be electronically turned so I could face the floor and have my bed sheets changed, all without disturbing my new grafts. I said goodnight to everyone as I guessed it was around 11:00PM, when Liz and Eddie typically got off their shifts and Doris came in to begin hers.

I was losing my modesty more each day I bathed in front of Marvin or Eddie. Fortunately, neither one of them behaved inappropriately when I had to be stripped down to nothing in the bath or bed. I couldn't say that about every male caregiver I ever encountered.

"Your butt cheeks are hanging out." My mother told me as she walked in for lunch the day after I came out of surgery. The mattress beneath me on the circular bed had a hole in it, big enough for a bedpan to slide into from below. If the bedpan wasn't there, my bare butt cheeks hung out through the hole. It is still strange to think how little personal privacy of patients was valued in the hospital.

She told me to make sure a sheet could be draped enough over the sides of the bed to cover my naked posterior as she fed me meatloaf and mashed potatoes. Keeping my butt covered became a low priority in the burn unit as I could not move and everyone around me never stopped.

I don't remember how I passed the hours that week in bed. I suppose like all teenagers I could kill time without thinking about it or I struggled with how slow time moved. Unfortunately, I didn't consider my required stillness a spiritual practice at seventeen. I saw it as a means to an end, a passage through, and when I got to the end of the tunnel, the light I reached would be my healed body and my escape from the prison of hospitalization.

I had no choice but to call someone when I needed the bedpan if it wasn't already attached to my bed, and ask that same person to wipe me when I was finished. Needless to say, I waited till I couldn't tolerate it anymore before I called for the bedpan.

"Is that the way you wipe your own ass!" I yelled at dear, sweet Doris one night after she had patiently tolerated having to do something she enjoyed less than I did. I felt ashamed and embarrassed as soon as I said it. She didn't strike back at me the way Becky would have and that's why I probably yelled at her, I knew she was safe and would respect my anger, even though my anger had nothing to do with her.

Doris was a few years older than me and always worked graveyard shift. "I like it because it's quieter and I don't feel like I've wasted the day when I go home, and besides, it pays time and a half." She smiled sweetly at me like I was a normal person, not the crippled freak others like Bruce on the outside saw when they looked at me with grief-filled eyes. "I want to be a model and it takes daytime hours to find that kind of work." She had milk chocolate brown skin, large brown eyes, and was thin, like Diana Ross, and when I told her who she reminded me of, she smiled without any of the vanity I assumed women like her had. She pulled a chair up against the side of my bed and just talked to me on the late nights when I couldn't fall asleep and was a model of feminine strength before I knew there was such a thing.

If one stood off to the side of me in my bed, the silver, metal frame was a huge circle and the mattress-covered board where I laid perfectly still, face up, its seven-foot diameter and my protruding butt cheeks, its center. I wondered how they got that seven foot wide circle into my small room and decided that was one reason for partition walls that could be moved when necessary.

Every morning, when it was time to change my sheets, I would be turned from face up to face down, slowly, by the motor attached to my bed that sounded like a forklift. Before any turning began, a mattress covered board the same size as the one beneath me would be placed on top, making me a human sandwich for the next few minutes. I would be reminded again and again to remain perfectly still, which I accomplished after a few days. Halfway around, with my body vertical, I could feel a board supporting my foot and I was told to let the board hold my weight. My arms were anchored to more boards that stayed parallel to the floor and I looked like Jesus on the cross, halfway around to fresh sheets. I looked forward to every morning I could be turned onto my stomach without being scolded for moving and reminded for the hundredth time how the entire grafting operation along with the week of catatonic recovery would be repeated if these grafts did not take.

I became a captive audience to every lousy show and the occasional entertaining show on the television that someone decided I should be watching. At each meal, a nurse, my mother or father would feed me like a baby, one spoonful at a time, one swallow at a time. "I can't eat that fast." I said to Delores as she tried to hurry me through breakfast one morning. She had other work to do, she reminded me, so she would walk from nurses' station to my bed every five minutes, so I could have time to chew and she could get something done.

Around day two of my perfect stillness, Kathy walked up to my left side, bent over, lifted up the sheet to look at my donor site on my abdomen, then without a word, pulled the mesh covering off with a single jerk.

"OWWWW!!" I yelled at her.

"I'm sorry, I should have told you before I did that." She sounded sincere.

"Yes." I agreed. "You should have told me before you did that."

"It looked a little oozy, so I'm going to get you a new bandage. Be right back." She lumbered out of the room.

She came back with bandage and a metal frame in the shape of a half-cylinder. "We can put this over your midsection to keep the sheets from sticking to your spots that are still healing.

Want to try it?" Anything that promised reduced pain I was willing to try. My father playfully referred to the metal frame as "the doghouse" which it did resemble placed over my trunk.

When my mother visited me at lunch she fed me and asked me about the previous twenty-four hours. My father would do the same at dinner. "Just lying around healing." I would say which would make at least one of us laugh. We laughed with joy because we knew we were getting closer to the goal of recovery and one day leaving all this pain behind us.

Kathy came to my bed on day eight, exactly at 7am, and told me she needed to check the grafts to see how they looked. Dr. Wray and one of his medical students came in as she unrolled a bit of bandage on my arm.

"Looks good. Let's see some further up." Dr. Wray said to Kathy as all three of them remained concentrated on the areas uncovered. "Wonderful!" Dr. Wray announced. "Ann, your grafts have taken beautifully! You can move again too. Are you excited?"

"Yeah." I said, still groggy, unaware of the significance of what he was saying. I attempted to shift first my back, then my arms and legs. My body from the neck down felt like the stiff boards I'd been attached to.

"Everything is going to get easier from here on out." Dr. Wray spoke with such enthusiasm, I wanted him to give some of that energy to me. "I'll come by later on to see how you're doing." He turned and nearly jogged out the door with his side-kick resident two steps behind him, off to make his rounds with other patients all over the hospital.

All of the doctors and nurses had been telling me for weeks that when the grafts took and I saw skin on what was once my exposed layer of fat that looked like bloody hamburger meat, I would feel euphoric. They were right and by that first evening I was able to move, I felt high on something wonderful. There was no more painful peeling to be done! Liz and Eddie tucked me into bed lovingly as I declared them my favorite nurses ever.

I was able to sleep on my stomach for the first time in six weeks! Eddie offered to give me a back rub. Eddie was older than my parents, but a handsome, muscular man who never wavered from his sweet, gentle nature. I moaned like Floyd while his strong brown hands rubbed my back till I fell asleep. I slept through the night without drugs, for the first time in the hospital.

We heard rumors that the burn unit would soon close since all of the patients were well enough to either go home or be moved to a regular surgical floor. "It's true." Liz told me when I asked her one morning. "Whenever we can, we like to give the burn unit a good scrubbing so it's good and sterile for the next patients and to give the staff a break from intensive care work. One of us will follow you to the floor you're assigned and help you get adjusted. Don't worry, Ann." I didn't realize I looked so worried. I felt like a young bird being pushed out of the nest.

The night before we all left the burn unit, Floyd and I were soaking our bodies in the bath room, separated by a cloth divider. Floyd was moaning as usual and this time I decided to say something to him about it.

"What are you complaining about? If I were going home tomorrow, I'd be excited." I said, sounding like a chastising mother.

"You're right." He said, after a minute or two of silence. "I am lucky to be going home. And pretty soon, you'll be going home too Ann, just you wait and see."

"It's been something else in this place, Huh?" I said, not able to imagine what came next.

"Yes indeed...yes indeed." Floyd's voice trailed off. Each understood what the other meant and nothing else mattered in that moment.

Ann Kronlage

The next day, I don't remember saying goodbye to anyone as my mother pushed me in the wheelchair and Liz pushed a cart loaded with the few belongings I accumulated while in the burn unit. All of us who were burn survivors didn't want to continue a bond based on such pain and fear. The burn unit was a nightmare I couldn't shake from my memory soon enough, but of course I would never forget it. I just wanted to look ahead to a life I knew would be better.

Diving In Headfirst

CHAPTER 8 At fourteen years old, I charged off the three meter high diving board, challenging myself to soar as far forward as my body would carry me, hoping to get the attention of Carl, the sexy lifeguard and fellow swim team member. I propelled forward through the air, beyond the ten feet deep diving pool, not considering beforehand that I might reach the five feet deep swimming area. After I hit the surface of the water, I quickly struck the bottom of the pool with the top of my head, hearing the crunch of my skull, jaw, and neck as they slammed together. Underwater, sounds and thoughts reverberated in slow motion and I considered for a brief moment, the foolishness of my actions. Bringing myself to the surface of the water, I happily climbed up the ladder and out of the pool, right next to the lifeguard stand where Carl sat. I looked up at him to see if he had noticed my amazing dive. To my complete disappointment, both my dive and my presence escaped his notice. At least for a minute, until he looked down at me with a blank expression that quickly changed to shock as he said something about blood on my face and slowly climbed down from his stand. At this point I wouldn't have cared if my head was falling off, for I had his undivided attention, and he was holding me by the arm, walking me to the lifeguard locker room where the first aid supplies were kept. I looked around at the other people in the pool, and many of them had the same shocked look as Carl, whispering again about blood. I turned to look at Carl, hoping to find a spark of affection in his eyes, but he gripped my arm tighter and looked worried for reasons I couldn't understand. I was not concerned that I would bleed to death, or that I might have a fractured skull, or even a concussion. I only wondered how long I would be alone with him, imagining that he had just saved me from permanent injury. I felt woozy as he sat me down on a locker room bench, bandaging my head as he stood before me in his small spandex swimming suit, his sixteen year-old athletic body glistening inches away from my face. My injuries were not serious, although the doctor told my parents to check for concussion every two hours for the first twenty four hours afterwards, and of course in my mind it was worth it to get that close to Carl, whom I would never see again after that summer.

At an age when most of us felt like we would live forever, I experienced the power of that attitude as both dangerous and life-saving. A person who thinks she will live forever takes crazy risks like I did in front of Carl. A person who thinks she will live forever has the power of mind over body to survive experiences a negative attitude would not. The surgeons and nurses I met in the burn unit knew that. Looking back, I know it as well.

If my recovery in the burn unit was climbing up the ladder of the high dive, my two weeks on a regular surgical floor were walking out to the edge of the diving board.

My mother pushed me in the wheelchair and we followed Liz out the wing of the hospital that held the burn unit and into an elevator with gray dusty padding on the bottom half of dingy metal walls. When the doors closed, it smelled like the back of an open television set at my dad's TV repair shop. I imagined that if the walls, dust and metal could talk, they'd have many stories to tell. Out the elevator, we passed into a different building with clean, white walls and waxed off-white linoleum floor. People walked up and down the long corridor, most looking like they knew where they were headed. Some looked sad, some happy, some confused and some very focused.

Some carried themselves confidently like hospital employees and others looked like strangers in a strange land searching for a way out. I loved wondering about all of them. Many of them looked at my face then glanced down at my legs with sadness in their eyes. I felt an odd mixture of happiness and disappointment in knowing I had become a different person in the last two months.

After fifteen minutes of elevators and hallways, Liz turned and said, "This is it." She stopped at a nurses' station, asked if the room was ready for me then walked in the direction the female finger pointed. We followed her to the end of another hallway, the farthest room under the charge of a group of caretakers I would never know like I knew the burn unit nurses and doctors. My new room had a toilet with a normal bathtub in a small bathroom to the left as we entered.

"It's a semi-private room that you have all to yourself for now." Liz said. She pointed to the two beds and large window on the far wall that overlooked the park across the street. "The view is definitely an improvement over the one in the burn unit."

She looked relieved and sad to say goodbye.

My mother got on the phone and called my father to tell him my new room and telephone number. She talked excitedly about my new space with its beautiful view and a telephone I had all to myself. She laid in the bed opposite the one I chose by the window and declared it comfortable enough to take a nap on when she visited exhausted from working all night at the BMC (bulk mail center).

Visiting hours were 1PM-9PM. I could sleep as late as I wanted and have as many visitors as I wanted. No one would bug me about eating more food or inflict pain by pulling away dried on bandages. After my mother left, I savored the idea that my life seemed finally pointed in a direction toward normal.

An endless parade of unfamiliar faces came in and out of my "regular" room. Some nurses introduced themselves as they took my blood pressure and temperature and showed me how to call them on the buzzer or turn on the TV. Others were less friendly when they came to empty trashcans, sweep the linoleum floor or clean the bathroom. Others came to drop off a tray of food or take blood from my arm with barely a smile on their faces. I started to trust less and ask more questions of these people who didn't seem to want to get to know me the way everyone had in the burn unit.

Almost every morning I woke up to soft whispering at the foot of my bed. Dr. Ollinger smiled proudly as he introduced a new doctor beside him then asked me how I felt that morning. I didn't tell him I felt like a sideshow at the circus because he was so kind about his intrusion. Dr. Wray came by at irregular times without waking me up and looked just as proud. The doctors who knew me from the beginning constantly told me how well I healed. Every other day Marlene showed up with more splints and exercises that I could do to improve my range of motion. Most evenings, when I needed my bandages changed, Eddie lit up my evening with his warm gentle self. Someone had wisely decided that having a nurse familiar to me and to my wounds would help me recover better in my new environment. My bandages were no longer a source of extreme pain, but covering for my tender scars. His familiar face was reassurance I had come a long way.

Within a few days, I had a roommate in the bed by the door. Her name was Judy and she was there to have surgery on her eye. She was about the same age as my mother, didn't talk too much and didn't leave the TV on too much or too loud. Her husband Bob did enough talking for the both of them when he visited every evening at dinner. When he said he was a minister however, I decided to see if he had any answers to why God was punishing me.

"God is not punishing you. He loves you more because of your suffering. He doesn't give any of us anything more than we can handle." Bob preached like he was at the pulpit.

"How can you say this is love? People don't burn in hell because God loves them more. I can only understand this to be punishment and the only big sin I can remember committing is not going to church on Good Friday." I spoke with a hope that he could convince me otherwise. He continued to rattle off verses from the Bible and tell me what he believed and only convinced me that he had never had the question why haunt him the way it haunted me.

The next evening when Bob came to visit Judy, he stayed a little later, after the dinner trays were picked up.

Eddie came in, pulled the curtain around my bed and began helping me change my bandages. Eddie realized, after having uncovered my legs, that he needed a few more rolls of gauze and would go to the nurses' station in search of them. "You can air out for a few minutes, okay Ann?" he joked as he walked out the door.

Bob and Judy weren't talking much so I thought he might want to see a little more of what I was talking about when I asked why. "Hey Bob, wanna come over and see what my legs look like without the bandages?" I said. "I'm covered up above that but you should come see what I mean by punishment." I secretly enjoyed the idea that this was probably the worst thing this person who spoke for God had ever seen.

As he walked out from behind the curtain, he kept his eyes down at the foot of my bed where the remnants of my once athletic legs rested. I hoped for the first time that he would say something but he only studied them in silence. Bob stopped talking like a preacher after that, which both saddened and relieved me. Bob and I never discussed God again or possible answers as to why my injuries had happened.

One night a friend from school came to visit. Rick was a junior and a football player on the varsity team. He looked like a football player—solid as an old tree—but I knew him as a big teddy bear. Rick wore a traditional African man's tunic that seemed to give him a pride in his step I hadn't noticed at school. I felt hesitant to have anyone who hadn't seen me in the burn unit visit me in the regular room. Maybe he or she would not be able to hide the shock one must surely feel when seeing me for the first time, I told myself. Rick did not act shocked or disgusted, but only concerned. Ten years later, I was not surprised to hear that Rick went to medical school and became an MD.

After Rick left, Bob made a sarcastic comment that reminded me of something my father would say. "That's some kind of black man."

I looked at Bob for a second, trying to understand what he meant by that, not wanting to believe he was another of those idiot bigots like Archie Bunker on TV.

"He's my friend." I said, ready to argue about the stupidity of his comments. Bob looked away and said nothing further about Rick or anyone who came to visit me.

Within a few days, Judy had her surgery and went home. A few days later, as I was having my final minor skin graft surgery, I received a Get Well card from Judy and Bob, with a handwritten note wishing me a speedy recovery.

"What would you say to going home on Saturday?" Dr. Wray said to me as he looked me over one morning while Marlene waited to measure me for something.

"You're serious?" I studied his face to be sure. "You're not going to change your mind?" I asked.

"No!" He laughed tenderly. "Why would you say such a thing? I am completely serious. You can go home on Saturday. I'll write it in your chart, so make your plans to go home on Saturday morning." He patted my bed then rushed off to another patient.

"I have to call my family." I said to Marlene. She smiled and handed me the phone. My mother cried when I told her. My brother Louie sounded excited as though everyone at home would be waiting for me. I was really going home. My God, I was really going home. I heard Martin Luther King Jr.'s words 'Free At Last, Free At Last, Thank God Almighty I'm Free At Last.'

I can't stop smiling as my mother pushes me in the wheel-chair through hallways I can't remember, into elevators I thank under my breath, and across a lobby with carpet I remember from eight weeks earlier.

Automatic doors open and a gust of warm moist air blows across my face. There is something different about this air from outside. It is alive as I feel right now leaving the dark cave of the hospital.

I smell exhaust from tired city buses. I smell gasoline engines cough odors that remind me of Terry, a guy I went out with once, who loved to work on his car and carried evidence of such in his body odor.

I look at people move in every direction—down the side-walk, across the street, through the courtyard. A young mother holds her newborn baby, an old couple arm in arm, a woman about the age of my mother looks like a hesitant visitor.

I am so happy I can feel a smile stretch across my face. Some people look back at me with wide-eyed horror. I remember that I am different and I know this will not be the last time people react with shock at the sight of me. But I can't stop smiling. It is all too good to stop and I wonder why no one else has a smile that stretches across their faces. Then I see Louis.

My most stubborn rival of all my brothers and sisters, he and I fought so viciously, I thanked God every day I was twice his size. On this day of my newfound freedom, he stands before the celery green station wagon that my parents purchased while I was away. He holds open the door on the rear passenger side with a smile stretched across his face. I can't recall a time he looked happier.

As my mother pulls out of the hospital driveway, onto the main road, then onto the freeway, I am aware of every rock, every bump, and every crack the tires roll over. My mother and brother seem oblivious to sensations I feel throughout my body.

Then my mother turns the wheel down Coachlight Lane, where my family has lived for ten years.

"It's so green!" I say, as if I am seeing it all for the first time. The last time I saw Coachlight Lane it was mid-April. Now it is mid-June and green jumps out at me from everywhere but the blue sky. Louis turns around from the front seat and stares at me as I drink in the green splendor. My mother lets out a heavy, happy sigh.

"It's so green!" I had to say again with the hope someone else might enjoy it as much as I, as if to say 'Can't you see it?'

We pull onto the driveway. My mother turns off the car and tells me to wait while she goes inside to get the wheelchair she borrowed from Gerri, our back fence neighbor. Louie jumps out too and follows my mother into the house.

The neighborhood sounds the same as I remember it. Air conditioners and lawn mowers hum in the distance. A commercial jet shoots through the clouds and reminds me how close we are to the airport. Sprinklers spit out relief to both grass and children. The hot moist air vibrates with life. I do not want to go inside like everyone else living in this midday sauna.

"Oh Gussie!" My mother whispers as she hugs then helps me out of the car and into the wheelchair that Gerri found at a garage sale for ten dollars. My mother's face is wet with tears and perspiration she doesn't try to wipe away.

"Let me make you some nice lunch." My mother offers as

she pushes me into the kitchen. "Where would you like to eat, in here or on the front porch?"

"The front porch." I say without hesitation. She reminds me to stay out of the sun, which the doctors and nurses drilled into our heads the past few weeks.

I feel it again when I go outside, how alive the air is, like a giant set of lungs, inhaling and exhaling, nurturing all of this life with its warm breath.

The taste of the grilled cheese sandwich and glass of milk my mother delivers to me on a tray; the sound of birds; the children on bicycles racing by in pairs; the smell of freshly-cut grass; all of it is both familiar and extraordinary.

"Did you see your new bedroom?" My ten-year-old sister Martha asked me after she hugged me hello.

When I went into the hospital, my bedroom was in the basement in a room that had no windows but lots of privacy. While in the hospital, my family moved the contents of my bedroom to the bedroom at the front of the house, where two large vertical rectangular windows let in the afternoon light.

My mother replaced the worn orange shag carpeting with an emerald green carpet that matched the sheets and bedspread I chose for my previous birthday. She bought extra sheets and made curtains and upholstered a small chair placed lovingly between the two windows.

Before being injured I felt totally invisible to everyone in my family. After returning, every one of my siblings, from twenty-one year old Marie, to seven year old Tina, treated me like a precious addition to the household. My mother prepared every meal I ate, then placed it on a tray, which was then brought to me in my bedroom by one of my brothers or sisters. I could call out at any time of the day and someone would come to ask me if I needed something. I was not just special for a day, I was special for many months to follow. I had never experienced such treatment and I wasn't going to do or say anything that would cause it to end. My brothers and sisters left me alone when I wasn't asking for something to be brought to me and happily fetched whatever I requested. My parents would do anything I asked of them and I knew it. I was in teenage heaven—most of the time.

The morning after I came home from the hospital, my mother helped me into the bathtub. Without warning, she gasped, blurted out "You used to be so beautiful!" then rushed out of the bathroom, sobbing.

I sat quietly and wondered why she never told me I was beautiful. I always thought of myself as a bloated, amazon version of her, not beautiful as she recalled too late. It seemed we had both been robbed of something because of our beliefs about beauty. I felt sorry for her that she could not see the beauty in fighting for survival in a body that would not give up. I sat in that bathtub till the water turned cold, proud of how far I had come, protective of the fragile frame that tenaciously held me.

I couldn't separate myself from her physically, but from that day forward, I never thought of myself as a version of her. I was nothing like her. I wasn't going to fall apart over something that had already happened, that was useless to cry about and compare to the way things used to be. I would never be like her. I would never allow myself to hurt the way she was hurting.

A week later, my mother told me a man was on the phone asking to talk to me.

"Hello Ann, this is Ron James from the Army Recruiting Office. How are you today?" A man's voice spoke with feigned sincerity. How did he get my name I wondered till I remembered filling out some form at school that confirmed my interest in joining the Army. I didn't really care about learning to be a soldier, I just wanted to leave my parents' house as soon as possible.

Ann Kronlage

"Fine, how are you?" I waited for him to proceed.

"Great. How's your summer going?" He sounded like such a charged up salesman, I knew I was going to enjoy dropping the bomb on him.

"My summer's pretty good so far. I just got out of the hospital. It was rough for a while, after my left leg was amputated, but I'm doing much better now." I listened for a reaction.

"Oh. I'm sorry to hear about that. Oh. I'm sorry to have bothered you....

Goodbye." He didn't wait for me to say goodbye before he hung up.

I was glad to so easily get rid of him but unnerved by an attitude that I would confront again and again in those who let fear guide them.

"We were so amazed that you never cried out loud those few weeks after the hospital." My mother said to me twenty years later.

I believed that if I started to cry everyone would react with such despair that the only thing crying out loud would accomplish was a great weight of depression. I sensed depression lurked just outside my room and that no one was capable of protecting me from it, so I vowed to protect myself by emotionally separating from anyone who wasn't totally optimistic about me.

I wanted desperately for my parents to protect me and to tell me what to do, but I knew they couldn't resolve their own fears about what lay ahead for me. Had I not been rebellious, I think I would have drowned in depression and fear about the future. Perhaps it is true what I had been told in the hospital—God does not give us any more than we can handle. I am grateful that my parents were who they were, for without them as a mirror to my search, I would not be able to tell you what I understand today. I needed them to challenge my expression so my convictions could be tested and thus strengthened.

My father came home from work that first night and into my room. "It's so nice to have you home again." He said with tears in his eyes.

"Yeah." I said "I don't know if it's so great to have this wheelchair to try and get around in. It's almost too big for the hallway. I need to go to the bathroom." I adjusted myself in the chair and maneuvered toward the doorway.

"Let me help you with that." My father said as he stepped behind me and pushed the wheelchair.

"Liz at the hospital told me I should try and do as much for myself as possible." I said confidently.

"Oh…okay." He sounded confused then hurt by my rejection. Before my injuries, I never could have spoken so honestly to my father without a slap in the face. Now I was telling him to stop and he respected my request. He walked out of the room with a heavy head drooped in front of him.

The first Sunday at home became my first time back to Mass. On crutches with one foot gone, there was no mistaking me for anyone else. For some reason I was seated in the first pew with my family and told to not get up for Communion like everyone else, rather to stay seated and the priest would bring Communion to me. I felt like an old lady, a pathetic invalid, a person that the world was giving up on. Looking around at all the people looking at the priest as he spoke, all I could see was fear. Fear of being different, fear of not getting it right, fear of being punished. Maybe that's what they all thought of me, that I was now different and being punished for not getting something right. I was so remarkably different that it was uncomfortable to look at me but it was so unbelievable that one couldn't help but stare. I wanted to jump up and scream the way I had in the hospital. I wanted to run from this hypnosis called religion but I also felt scared that maybe I got it wrong or that if I run I will be alone for the rest of my miserable life.

Mutilated ideals are what I saw when I looked at a magazine ad, watched a television commercial, or listened to a young man's description of a perfect woman. Every one of these glimpses into the values of my culture, previously standards for me to aspire to, became piercing stabs in my heart. If I wanted to live, I needed to turn away from those images of the media and commit myself to asking the question "Is this something that will cause you to feel good about yourself or bad about yourself?" I cleaned out a closet of worries in my mind that I decided were ideas that only led me to feel bad about myself. Changing my attitude saved my life and I found hope and joy in the empowerment of my thinking.

I decided any aspirations to attract a boyfriend would lead to feeling bad about myself, so I threw that idea out of my worry closet too. In letting go of my worries about attracting a boyfriend, I began to ask myself "What do you want? What is important to you?" This decision to ignore all of the external voices gave me a marvelous freedom to be who I wanted to be. I wanted to have fun and be fun, so I made a conscious decision to avoid complaining about anything in front of people. Unless I had some power to change a circumstance, I had little reason to complain. I had always found complainers to be boring at best, aggravating at worst and the most effective people repellents. Feeling good about myself did not include being a people repellent so unnecessary complaining was another thing I tossed out of my worry closet.

As one friend after another visited me at home, I felt the huge distance between them and me. Linda, Rebecca's step sister, talked about her horny boyfriend who couldn't keep his hands off her and the sunburn she got while making out with him behind the handball courts. Before the hospital, I would have laughed her story off, wishing I could find a horny boyfriend to obsess about me. This time her stories of lust and pain had me imagining myself at the edge of a cliff, with Linda's voice yelling out to me to jump. She was safely on the ground and wanted me to join her, along with many of our other mutual friends. "I can't jump, it's too dangerous!" I yelled back to her.

As I listened to her talk about how her bra strap pushed too tightly on her delicate red skin, I wanted to tell her that a sunburn is just a first degree burn, that her skin will soon heal itself and she will forget all the pain and inconvenience. But I knew if I said that I would sound like a complainer about my hard life and no one would want to visit me and I would be alone and I didn't want to be alone. So I listened to Linda talk about her carefree life as if she wished it were a soap opera.

How was it that I had become so truly different from these people I called friends a couple of months earlier? Was it that I had seen both the beginning and the end of life crash into one another? Like when one barely misses a major collision and realizes she is still shaking from the fear. I was still shaking while my friends slept through the near crash in the back seat. I could try to explain to them what I saw but how could they ever understand?

I could take what those like Linda said as absolute truth and feel competitive with her and allow myself to drop off the edge of the cliff. But I refused to feel bad about myself. I knew I didn't want to die. I didn't want to give up. I couldn't imagine giving up, but I could see the opportunity waiting for me to give up, like the abyss over the edge. It was right there in front of me. It was exhilarating and terrifying to be so close to it. I was pulled between pretending none of this ever happened and accepting I could never be the same.

The Olympics were on television all day long for several weeks. My favorite sport to watch was gymnastics. The first to get a perfect score of 10, Nadia Comaneche, showed up that summer on the television. I watched transfixed as did so many others. My father and Rebecca's reaction, when I asked the next day to turn the channel to the Olympics, was to discourage me from viewing that which I would never be able to do. Did they think I could have done even a fraction of any of it before being injured? What kind of stupid reasoning did people perpetuate in what could only be explained as fear?

"Father Denny wants to come visit you." My mother came into my room explaining one late morning. "I shouldn't say Father anymore, he's just Dennis Donner. You heard he quit being a priest last year didn't you?" My mother enjoyed being in the center of gossip more than why Father Denny decided to visit me, it seemed. She told him to come over anytime so he asked how about in an hour? "I told him okay. I could call him back if it's not, but I thought you wouldn't mind."

"That's fine Mom." I said. I always liked Father Denny. He had such a gentle, generous spirit when he led the youth group at our church. Rumors went around about why he had left the priesthood the following year and no one had seen him since.

When he walked into my room after my mother met him at the front door, I knew instantly that the rumor that he had had a nervous breakdown was true. His eyes were the part of him that had changed. They did not reveal the warm, loving soul I knew from before. His had become the eyes of a deeply wound-ed creature who literally looked like he had just seen a ghost. He had come to offer me hope in my struggles. I thanked him and wished him the same. He said goodbye with a hug after a few minutes and I never saw him again.

When I first came home from the hospital I was given a wheelchair to use for getting around. It was time for senior pic-tures, so my mother loaded me and chair into the car and drove us to the photography studio where attempts would be made to present me as a normal seventeen year old in front of a camera. I told my mother to stay in the car. I needed help getting through the entry door then the waiting room where about ten uncomfortable young faces stared as it became obvious my chair was too wide. "Alright everybody stand up and push your seats over to make room for her." The man in charge announced. I shrunk from the embarrassment but luckily it was my time to escape to the back where pictures were taken. On the way home I asked my mother for something besides a wheelchair. She got a walker for me. Too slow, I decided. How about crutches, she offered. That was it for me. A pair of wooden crutches with adjustable height and hand rests. It felt good to stand straight again, even if I still stood on one foot. With crutches I could fit through tight spaces, jump over things in my way or pull myself up from the floor. Crutches gave me a fun, physical challenge the way sports did. Crutches were an extension of my legs, my arms and easy to bring along whenever I traveled in the car.

That summer after the hospital, I discovered that when I expected nothing, everything was good. I didn't worry about making up the six weeks of school I missed. The principal told me I didn't have to make it up because I was a straight-A student for several semesters before that. I didn't worry that I'd be stuck in the house with my friends all out having summer fun without me. They came to me and soon were driving me around.

Rebecca was the one with the family car one afternoon, so she drove where she wanted to go. She didn't ask too many "Where do you guys want to go?" questions because she knew where she wanted to go and that was always faster than waiting for Jane, Laura and me to agree. Roger's house was Rebecca's first choice that day.

Roger was a handsome freshman who visited me once in the burn unit. When he visited me a second time he came with my father to my semi-private room. I don't know who he surprised more, me or my father, when he French kissed me goodbye. I loved Roger for his unconventional behavior. He was a wonderful combination of normal jock who played by the rules and irreverent teenager who experimented with whatever caught his attention.

Rebecca stopped the station wagon in front of Roger's house, laid on the horn and yelled "Hey Roger!" when he appeared at the front door. Roger came out, leaned into Rebecca's window and managed to flirt with the four of us simultaneously. Roger was one of those guys who loved women and was loved by women.

Soon Roger's friends Dale and Darren came from down the street to join him. Darren was a tall, thin goofy-looking kind of guy and Dale was shorter and a ruggedly handsome guy I remembered seeing in the halls at school. Dale carried his six-foot long pet snake with him. Even Rebecca acted coy about touching a live snake.

Roger became one of the regular visitors at my house. He usually brought Dale and Darren with him. Rebecca began showing up when Roger arrived, sometimes with Jane or Laura. We gossiped, laughed and sang to the music on my 8-track player. I remembered what it was like to be a carefree teenager again.

The fourth of July was in a few days. This was no ordinary fourth of July. It was the big bicentennial celebration across the United States. Everywhere one looked, Bicentennial this and Bicentennial that followed. It was like Christmas, but dragged on in sweltering summer heat. And just like Christmas had been for most of my life, I was somewhat disappointed, somewhat relieved as I sat on the hood of my parents' station wagon and watched the fireworks spray the dark sky with color and light.

After Roger stopped visiting, Dale continued to visit, every day. He stayed for hours; sometimes a few, sometimes eight or nine, till the dark summer sky told us both we needed to say goodbye. My mother made him lunch or dinner or both if he was there. He told me about his family and one by one he met each of seven siblings and parents. I was glad to have a friend to pass the time with. I didn't regard Dale as a prospective boyfriend since he told me he had a girlfriend. I didn't feel he treated me like he was interested in romance, but I was very inexperienced when it came to romance.

I was happy to have Dale as a friend. One day when another friend Sherlyn came over, she flirted with him and I felt a twinge of jealousy and checked to see if he flirted back. He didn't, I saw with relief. Happiness became silliness and I began to hop around my bed on the only foot I had. Sherlyn joined me as Dale watched and we giggled like little children. I lost my balance but Dale caught me with a firm hold on my hips. Sherlyn and I both realized he was flirting with me! I was the scarred up, one-legged one and he was flirting with me? I pushed it aside in my mind, it was so hard to believe.

He was interested in me? I always thought teenage guys wanted physically perfect girls they could get lucky with and laughed at the ones not physically perfect. I always felt like someone that guys laughed at and since being burned I felt utterly undesirable in the eyes of any teenage boy. Dale would change that forever.

Poised

On the last day of any dive vacation, the day before one boards the plane back home, the best advice is to stay out of the water as far as scuba is concerned. The body needs time to recover between the pressure changes of diving and the imminent pressure changes of flying. Often, divers departed on Sundays to the airport back home so the dive shop offered a snorkeling trip on Saturdays to satisfy the collective urge to get in the water. Sandi and I were two of the collective on our last day in the Bahamas. Our new friend Bill, whom we met during the week diving, also signed up for snorkeling that morning.

On a spacious pontoon boat we took off with the lightness of only fins, masks and snorkels. Bill and I had slept together the last three nights in his room. Sandi and I both flirted with Bill and he with each of us. He lived in Florida, we in Missouri. For me it was a strange mixture of wanting to get closer to him but not wanting to get hurt by our impending separation. I also had a wave of insecurity that morning that screamed Why would an attractive, educated man like him be interested in me for a long term relationship? In other words, I told myself, keep your emotional distance in order to minimize the pain upon tomorrow's goodbye.

As the saying "better be careful what you wish for" goes, my inner intention manifested to an outer action. The three of us fell into the water and floated on our stomachs with our masked faces submerged, scanning the shallow bottom with our eyes. I even wore my prosthetic leg since it didn't hinder me at the surface the way it did at the bottom. Our boat had anchored in a cove with little boat traffic around on a cloudy afternoon. Compared to the week's diving, we didn't have to worry about anything going wrong. So when I looked around after ten minutes and noticed that Bill and Sandi had turned in a different direction, out of earshot, I decided to continue for ten more minutes on my own, then head back to the boat after that.

What did I expect from a guy I hardly knew? To stay by my side forever? Stop feeling sorry for yourself and enjoy the little bit of vacation you have left, I told myself. Look, over there, a barracuda all by its lonesome. I'd seen many barracuda in the Cayman waters, always waiting under the shadow of the boat we left then came back to after our group dives. I never felt scared of barracuda in that situation because it seemed as though they weren't waiting for us as their prey, just enjoying the shade of the boat as camouflage from other unsuspecting creatures lurking about. That is how I first regarded the Bahamas barracuda until I noticed its mouth was gaping in my direction as if it prepared to charge at me. I certainly couldn't swim away fast enough to escape this torpedo-shaped fish. Knowing that fish were attracted to motion, I looked at my body and noticed my white legs kicking. Stop kicking I told my legs. In the salt water your body just quietly floats when you stop moving. I did that and watched as the barracuda closed its mouth and swam away.

I made my way back to the boat, thanking my guardian angel and any other spirit responsible for my quiet rescue. Unfortunately my parting with Bill the next morning was not as gracious as with the barracuda. Assuming that no respectable men like him could be seriously attracted to someone like me, I pretended to not care about him as he walked away from my cold goodbye.

Six weeks had passed since I left the hospital. Four weeks had passed since Dale began visiting me daily.

"I am going to kiss you at five o'clock." Dale announced one afternoon. I didn't argue with him. We sat face to face, nervously, for the next half-hour. I talked about people we both knew, about the '76 Olympics that summer, about my brothers' and sisters' annoying personalities, but I only thought about what it would be like to kiss him. He was a very good kisser, I discovered. Dale was an answer from God when I expected only anger and punishment.

Within a few days, we turned off the lights in my bedroom and laid on the floor; necking and exploring each other with our hands. Within thirty minutes, my father opened the door without knocking, took a few steps inside and saw us quickly sit up in the dark room. Without a word, he immediately turned back around, stepped out of the room and closed the door. That was an incredible sight for me to behold—my father made speechless at the sight of me with a boyfriend. Less than a year earlier, a boy I knew had come to our front door to pick me up for a date. My father's reaction then was to stand at the large picture window beside the front door, with four or five of my siblings imitating him, and giggle at the sight of me walking away with my date. I didn't know what to do with my father's discomfort with my dating, except to hide my interest in the opposite sex around my family.

Dale changed things. My parents both liked Dale. He cared for me at a time when they didn't expect tenderness to come from any teenage boy. I watched, awestruck as Dale wooed them and me more each day.

Rebecca, Jane, and some others asked me to go with them to the drive-in one evening and I asked Dale to come too. He said he would have to break off completely from his girlfriend Diane, who still had a ring he gave her. I went to the drive-in that night without Dale.

The running gag at the drive-in that my girlfriends and I

pulled was to see how many of us could get in for free while still in the car. In other words, how many of us could hide, usually in the trunk. We all laughed about how freaked out people would act at the sight of my amputated leg, so I proposed an idea that would take advantage of that. One of us could lie on the floor of the car with a blanket over her and my feigned sleeping pathetic self on top of that. We gambled that the person counting heads at the entry booth wouldn't dare ask me to move, so unnerved would he or she be at the sight of my leg. It was true, I wasn't asked to move and we saved an extra $2.00 which we spent on food at the concession stand.

Dale came to me the next day with a look of relief on his face. "We are officially broken up." He declared then pulled the ring out of his pocket. "I can go with you to the drive-in or anywhere else with a clear conscience from now on." It felt like the most romantic thing that a guy had broken up with someone else to be with me.

Dale and I became known as a dating couple. I loved the look on some faces that silently asked "What is he doing with her?" I sat back and relaxed for the rest of the summer and enjoyed surprising everyone as much as I had been surprised by young love.

Dale would show up at my front door every day at about 10. He was really funny and he loved to play Scrabble with me. He was my prince charming because with him I could focus on other issues like taking care of myself. We were wonderful conversationalists together.

One evening as we sat in my bedroom, all alone except for the whirring fan in front of us, relieving the stifling humidity and heat of a typical Missouri August, Dale suggested he return later that same evening.

"How are you going to do that without anyone noticing?" I asked, loving the adventure of him and his idea.

"Grandma's asleep in the next room, the fan's running and I will quietly slip through this window. No one will know. What do you say?" He spoke to my neck as he gently kissed it.

My grandma, my mother's mother, the one that used to take my bed when she visited, was next door to me in my sister Susan's bed. He was right, she wouldn't notice, particularly because she snored ferociously. Because I knew Grandma would really be upset if she found out and I was curious about losing my virginity and felt absolutely safe with Dale, I agreed.

Dale left at his usual time, about 10PM, through the front door, with our secret plan in place. At midnight, I would remove the screen on the casement window and he would slip in and into bed with me.

One of my recovery rituals was wearing a body stocking on the top half of my torso and arms. Every night my mother helped me get my arms into the tight stocking that was suggested to help flatten my skin grafts. This big night was no exception. I wondered if I would be a turnoff for Dale. I apologized as I let him in. He kissed his way through the window. At seventeen I was the virgin while Dale at fifteen was the experienced one. How was your first time? The first time for me was odd, like slipping into a pair of blue jeans that were a bit too small. Dale held me gently and whispered I love you in my ear.

The last week of August was the beginning of my senior year of high school. I was nervous at the idea of facing over 2000 people who had only known me as an athlete and straight-A student and would now see me as what? I was thirty pounds lighter, including ten inches of left leg removed, and my arms and face were pink with burn scars. I traveled on crutches since the orthopedic surgeon said I was not ready to be fitted with a prosthetic leg. Whenever I went out in public, like to the movies with Dale or a restaurant with my family after church, I felt like a tarnished celebrity. The expression on each stranger's face was pity, fear and/or morbid fascination. People sometimes never bothered to look me in the eye they were so distracted by the rest of my body. I felt anger on top of sadness that everyone who saw me had an opinion that he/she did not hesitate to express with wide gawking eyes. The few people who did speak to me of my injuries always responded with "You're lucky to be alive!" which infuriated me for years. I was a teenager having trouble with resolving my own feelings about all that had happened. To be looked at with pity and sadness then told I was lucky screamed hypocrisy to me. Everywhere I turned the hypocrisy faced me, like the body I now lived in that could not be ignored. Other people could hide their scars of alcoholism, etc. that never came to the surface but not me. I was stuck as I saw it with having to face my scars and even wear them on my outside for all the world to judge. As the years went by and I became more comfortable and proud of myself, people's reactions to me shifted as well. I didn't know it then but would later come to understand that because of all that I really was lucky.

High school, where everyone knew me and my story as it circulated the previous spring while I was in the hospital, was easier because the question of "What happened to you?" was not constantly posed. I felt much less nervous knowing that Dale would be by my side from the time I entered the building till I left after eighth period. He must have tolerated looks and comments from people I never knew about and the subject only came up once between us. He told me a guy named Don snickered and made some kind of stupid remark after I had passed and within earshot of Dale as he followed me. Dale was used to standing out in the crowd from the time he was in grade school because he had a condition that made him look like an adult at a premature age. By high school he looked like everyone else and no longer had to endure the teasing that toughened him over the years. He was the perfect boyfriend for me at the time—tough enough to stand up to the attention I got and able to help me deal with the craziness of it all. When Don teased Dale about his different looking girlfriend. Dale told me he walked calmly over to the table where Don sat, and threatened to toss Don across the room if he ever said anything like that again. Don must have believed what Dale told him because he never said another word to either of us that year.

I cruised through my first three years of high school as a disciplined and motivated student. Back then, I believed if you worked hard enough for something, you could get it. Being a straight-A student seemed normal to me. My mother commented that anyone could get good grades at the public schools when I showed her my report card. I stopped bothering to show her after a few times. I believed myself to be ordinary except during the times I stood with other straight-A students for a photograph that was put in the school newspaper, or when someone reacted with amazement that I got straight–A's.

My physical therapy was called occupational therapy, which is therapy for small muscles like the ones in my hand. My left hand was still very weak and numb and I traveled thirty minutes by car to the hand rehabilitation clinic next to the hospital where I was a patient in the burn unit. Dale always accompanied me and was fun to hang out with, where I met with Marlene and sometimes others for sessions to return strength, range of motion and sensation to my left hand. Without strength I could barely pick up or hold onto anything, including telephones, door handles and so many other things we all take for granted unless our hands stop working. Sensation is very important too, I found out. My left hand was often cold as a result and one time I even tried to warm my hand under warm water. The warm water became scalding hot but I couldn't sense it and only after I had blisters did I realize how dangerous a loss of sensation can be.

After my injuries, grades were not important to me. One of my classes that fall of my senior year was Physics. The things the teacher, Ms. Miller talked about were interesting to me but I quietly remained in the corner of the room, pretending not to be interested. I noticed as she made her way around the room, responding enthusiastically to those students who acted the way I had in the past—eager to learn with most of the correct answers. I withdrew all semester from the pursuit of learning anything in Physics and escaped with a grade barely above an F. I wondered why no one, including my impossible-to-please mother, chastised me for such an embarrassing grade.

Occasionally Dale and I would decide to skip an entire day of school. We sat for hours in front of his old black and white TV, more interested in the long Scrabble games we played and peanut M&Ms that sustained us till his brother or sisters came home from school. By midmorning, Dale's phone rang with someone from the school attendance office asking what reason he had for his absence. Dale answered the phone with a scratchy voice, explained that he was sick and handed me the phone if someone asked to speak to his parent. No one questioned my authenticity as a concerned mother over the phone. We both delighted in the idea that we had gotten away with something. In the back of my mind I wondered why no one had called my house. No one ever chastised me or gave me detention for missing school the way my friends had been given detention for skipping school. I also got grades I didn't deserve from teachers I sensed felt sad for me.

The previous spring, when I made the cut at varsity cheerleading tryouts, then three days later was in the hospital with an amputated leg, the question of my status as a cheerleading lay in the back of everyone's mind. Of course I was still a cheerleader everyone told me to my face, but the thought of just standing before a crowd was something I avoided. I went to the football games with Dale, sat in the bleachers and pretended I never made or cared about cheerleading. It was enjoyable to just be outside on those beautiful Saturday afternoons. Next was basketball inside where once again Dale sat with me in the bleachers. I couldn't avoid the cheerleaders who greeted me and avoided the subject of whether I would return. I imagined what it could be like for me as a cheerleader. Ridiculous, I told myself and officially resigned my position for good. It wasn't as heartbreaking as I would have thought a year before had someone told me my future. I had a newfound patience for my body and felt proud of how far I'd come since Easter.

One day by myself, I stepped off an elevator where a young boy and his mother waited to get on. The boy gently said to me "You got your leg cut off?" to which I replied "Yes." with a smile. His mother quickly pulled him closer and told him to be quiet with an expression of embarrassment on her face and the two of them stepped into the elevator. I wanted to stop and explain to her that her son's reaction was the best kind I could ever ask for, but people seemed to move so quickly when they were nervous and I was a teenager still nervous about what people thought of me. It's ironic to me now as I write about it that at the time I wanted to embrace the innocent observations of children like that little boy and yet I wanted to be invisible as I had been before injury. Another way to explain it is I craved the intimacy of human contact but I feared the intimacy of human contact. But I was still growing, had shed my skin like a snake does before a growth spurt, and was just learning to feel comfortable in my new covering.

"You have severe nerve damage in your left hand." Dr. Wray explained to me. "Before any surgery can be done to repair the damage, we must assess the loss with a test involving an implement similar to a cattle prod which delivers a small amount of electrical impulse to your forearm and hand while measuring how far your nerve endings function. I'd like to set up an appointment for that test as soon as possible." I always liked his reassuring manner and this time was no different. I trusted him I told myself. Okay, let's do it, we agreed.

The hospital to which I returned, that had once been a prison for me, seemed transformed. Its large never-ending hallways were a comforting parent who told me "It's going to be okay, everything's going to be okay. You are no longer trapped, but are free to leave whenever you want." It was a place where I was most normal, most appreciated for my "amazing recovery".

On crutches without a left foot, I maneuvered proudly through the corridors with my mother and grandmother behind me. I studied each face I passed, some of them met my eyes and some of them looked longer at my asymmetrical legs. I longed for them all to see me as the courageous young woman the surgeons had, not the pitiful amputee so many eyes outside of the medical community had.

Suddenly, a familiar face from the past appeared. He was my swim coach from the summer I was fourteen. I knew he recognized me, but I could not make eye contact with him. I sensed his eyes quickly avoid mine. Hello, Tom, I wanted to say, but could not. His sad face hung heavier than I had ever seen it. Then I remembered. His sixteen year-old sister Sally had died less than a month earlier in a car accident. She and I swam on the relay team two summers before our accidents.

Beautiful Sally, the color of bronzed sunshine; the best butterfly swimmer I had ever known and Tom, the proudest big brother I had ever seen. That summer I had known her, she bounced with every movement of her body. Fluid, buttery limbs with long, wheat-colored hair, joy emanated from every inch of her tanned fourteen year-old body. It was hard to believe she was gone, until I saw the sorrow carved in the hardness of his face. I was a double impact of pain for him—a reminder of his sister and a reminder of the horrors of injury.

When we arrived at the office of our destination, my mother and grandmother waited in the front area while someone escorted me to an exam room. A 10' by 10' space with predominantly white coloring, it felt as if I had entered an empty closet with a table and metal box in storage. The woman who brought me in asked me to lie down on the padded table draped with a fitted sheet. She explained about the procedure with words similar to Dr. Wray's, as she held up the fragile looking probe that would become the center of our attention. I confirmed that I understood when another woman stepped into the room. She introduced herself in a way that made it clear hers was the senior position.

They began by taking a baseline measurement of my right arm. The probe was placed at my elbow while the assistant pushed a button on the metal box. My arm jumped in reflex, as I felt the electricity shoot through it. The probe was placed at my wrist, the button was pushed, and my hand jumped as I felt the electricity travel the shorter distance to the tips of my fingers. Interesting, I casually thought to myself. They moved to the left arm, beginning at the elbow. This time I felt the electricity travel down the length of my arm, but not to the tips of my fingers, stopping somewhere around the end of my palm. Then a thought flashed through my mind as suddenly as the surge passed through my arm—this was just a small dose of the force that nearly killed me months earlier. I panicked with a dead stillness as my vision became blurry, and I felt tears roll down my face. I wanted to run away from that terrifying white space, but I knew I could not. My tears gushed from a shattered floodgate deep within me. I heard one of the women ask me if I was okay. I mumbled about my association with this and past electric shocks as I sobbed. They did not seem able to offer a response, only a large box of white tissues. I wiped away rivers of grief-filled memories I hadn't known my body carried.

I dragged my stunned, exhausted body with shaky wooden crutches, down the short hallway to rejoin my mother and grandmother. My mother sounded worried as she wondered aloud if what she heard was indeed me crying. I nodded my head as I explained the memory trigger my body could not ignore. She let out her characteristic sigh of hopeless pity, which always felt like someone offering me a defective life preserver while I desperately fought to keep myself above water. My grandmother, like the women in the exam room, did not utter a sound. My mind imagined both mother and grandmother as giant sieves, unable to contain the weight of my tears, trapping only a few drops of my grief that would soon fall away.

I began to allow myself a good cry about once a month. I exercised control about my emotions the rest of the time and noticed how they came and went without any apparent reason. When a wave of sadness hit one day, I practiced telling myself that it would only last for maybe three days then be gone. My family allowed me my feelings as never before so this worked out well. Did I learn this recognition of my feelings in the hospital? Was this an answer to my prayers for understanding? All could be true and for it I am grateful.

One month later I returned to a different office in the hospital. The orthopedic surgeon, a short, stout, middle-aged woman named Dr. Badger examined my legs. "Are you ready to be fitted with a prosthetic leg?" she asked cheerfully. Of course I was I told her. She introduced me to a man not much older than I who was a double amputee. He had been in a car accident that crushed the lower part of both legs. He became a prosthetist, or someone who makes prosthetic limbs.

I became so excited at the idea of having two legs again. It required several visits to the prosthetic lab, where they measured my "stump" as people insisted on calling it, then the leg in progress, then the way I walked across the room using the handrails. Even my seven year-old sister Tina jumped around the house in excitement the first time I walked through the front door with my new leg on. I don't think she really understood the significance of my newfound mobility, but sensed the excitement in the nine older family members around her.

My prosthesis felt like a stilt the first time I walked on it. I couldn't feel the ground directly under my new left foot, which took several months to get used to. I tried physical therapy for a couple of sessions, which someone suggested would help me learn to walk. I stopped physical therapy, which seemed too slow and time consuming and started taking to the sidewalks with Dale every day.

I watched people walk everywhere I went. I wanted to have a natural, graceful gait. Heel to toe was the way the physical therapists said normal gaits looked like. Every day, from my house to Dale's, or from his house to mine, he and I walked hand in hand. He made me laugh and let me lean on him when I thought I would trip over my stiff-ankled left foot. His patience and encouragement helped transform me into a young woman with pride in my step.

Within the next few weeks, Dale and I went to the Homecoming Dance at our high school. I felt as though pants held my leg on better, so he and I decided to wear matching powder blue, polyester pantsuits. We felt fashionable wearing such outfits in 1976. Twenty-five years later, my teenage daughter Annie got a good laugh when she looked at the picture of Dale and I posing, with my brothers Joey and Louis making faces in the background.

After Christmas, my father asked me one day. "Are you ready to go shopping for the new car I promised you?" He said the money to pay for it would eventually have to come out of the settlement from the electric company, which he expected to be final within the next year. Like any normal teenager, I was ready to agree to anything if it meant a new car for me. We both agreed on a white, 1977 Camaro with maroon interior. I couldn't think of any adult I knew who had a brand new car, much less a teenager who was given one to drive to school every day. Instead of my father driving me and any of my friends who came over in time to school I could now drive myself every morning to school. Rebecca's house was on the way to school, so I picked her up every morning. I never noticed that the same parking space at school was made available by rent a cops moving cones out of the way as my car pulled up. Ten years later, Mr. Linke, a Vietnam vet and principal with the toughest reputation, confessed to me. "I told them to save that spot in front for you every day. I felt you deserved such a privilege after all that you had been through."

Five months later, I graduated with my class on a warm June afternoon. When I heard my name called, I grabbed the hand offered to me and carefully climbed the steps to the stage set up on the football field. I worried about tripping till I finished descending the few steps on the opposite side with diploma in hand. I looked up and saw the majority of the crowd of about a thousand people clapping and standing for me. Dale took a picture of me looking as though I was embarrassed by all the attention.

August 16, 1977 is a day I will never forget. It was the day of settlement between me the plaintiff vs. Diversified Electric Company, the day Elvis Presley died and the day I was admitted to the hospital for another reconstructive surgery. Six months earlier I turned 18, so by law I could stand as the plaintiff suing for compensatory and punitive damages. I didn't know anything about fair monetary amounts for such things. I trusted my father to know.

Six months out of the hospital, after the lawyers for the defendant visited me at home and saw for themselves the extensive injuries my body incurred, they began proposing offers to settle out of court.

"An annuity for $50,000 per year for the next twenty years." Came the first offer. My father balked at the unreasonableness of such an offer.

"$450,000 in cash." Came the next offer. My father appeared impressed as he told me.

"I told them you were rejected by your prom date, so they offered $20,000 more. I think we should take it." He told me with gleaming eyes. He and my mother wanted to keep it out of the courtroom and publicity by the media. The out of court settlement gave them what they wanted and me what I thought I was getting at 18—enough money to give me financial independence for the rest of my life. My parents' ignorance of the system and fear of endless delays and publicity pushed them to push me to agree to settle on the offer given.

I held up my right hand before the judge and swore to tell the truth. As a person six months past the age of majority, my agreement was required for the settlement to be official. I signed several documents, including my agreement to give up all future claims of injury against Diversified Electric. Today I regret having settled so quickly but back then I trusted my father's judgment on legal matters. He had begun taking classes in law at a night school. My family and I were lambs in the final steps before slaughter.

Someone handed me a check for $470,000 and I thought justice had been delivered. My parents and I drove home so I could pack for the hospital. Surgery on my leg was scheduled for the next morning. On my way out the door, my brother Louis stopped me and said. "Elvis Presley is dead!"

"You're lying!" I said. Elvis was only 42 years old. It sounded like something my brother would say to try and trick me for a good laugh.

Louis was not kidding that time though. Elvis really was dead.

Those few days away from Dale, as I stayed in the hospital, revealed to me his jealous nature. Bored with just sitting in my room all day long, I pushed myself around in the wheelchair and began a conversation with 16 year old Dan. We went to my room and ordered pizza and played with the channels on the remote. When Dale called later, we were eating our pizza and laughing at something on TV. Dale became furious that I had allowed "a stranger" in my room and demanded over the phone that I kick him out. I laughed at what I considered to be a ridiculous request. His anger escalated until I hung up on him. It shocked me that he couldn't trust me. He talked to me the way my father had before I was injured.

I started college in a nearby town, still living in my parents' house. By second semester I tried staying in the dorms. I wanted to experience living on campus as Rebecca had 125 miles away. I ate all my meals in the cafeteria, joined the social clubs, went to the Friday night showings of old movies where everyone howled with laughter, and even took a job as an overnight security dispatcher. I got bored with eating by myself most of the time, bored by the trivial concerns of young people who didn't know how lucky they were, tired of sitting alone at the movies because my boyfriend had to work that night and quit the dispatcher job after three days of trying to stay up all night and sleep during the day.

With the settlement money, my father helped me purchase a house down the street from my family. The first night alone in the house I couldn't sleep, the silence seemed so eerie. After a few days, I loved my independence and resisted Dale's attempts to move in or have a spare key to the front door. He began asking where I was and who I was with whenever he wasn't able to see for himself. I felt smothered by his jealousy and escaped any chance I could to Rebecca's college town where freedom and endless parties awaited me.

I made a deal with Dale that I would "try out" seeing other guys only in the college town where Rebecca lived and I visited every other weekend. Rebecca and I went to as many parties as our bodies could stand till we passed out or the sun came up. Where we went there was no evidence of young men and women looking for lifetime partners, only an endless parade of frat parties, sorority parties, apartment parties and happy hours at bars that changed names every semester. I felt grateful to climb into my white Camaro on Sunday afternoons after a long weekend of inebriation and drive home in peace and quiet with the gentle breeze through my open window soothing me back to normalcy. Each time I came back to Dale, I asked myself whether I was doing the right thing by breaking up with him. Each time his jealousy stung worse than any hangover, I knew breaking up was the right thing to do.

"If you break up with Dale, I think he might try to kill himself." Dale's mother said to me when I visited her one day. I mentioned this encounter to a counselor I trusted. He explained that if Dale were to commit suicide it wouldn't really be about me breaking up with him, but about many things in his life.

I wanted the jealousy to end so badly that I did things that were selfish and hurtful toward Dale. He always argued with or made fun of Rebecca, either behind her back or to her face. She was my closest friend and a strong advocate of promiscuous single life and an obvious huge threat to Dale and his desire to hang on to me. I understand now that what I wanted was for him to get mad at me and do the dirty work of breaking up so I wouldn't have to. By the time he received his diploma, two years after me, I knew he and I would not last if his jealousy continued.

"We have to break up. I can't take this anymore." I said to him as we stood in my unfurnished living room, arguing about whether I should go to Chicago with a bunch of female friends or stay home and be with him. I had no more tears left for a relationship that was past hurting but now destroying both of us if we let it continue. Dale didn't argue with me this time. He slowly descended the stairs into the basement and found a concrete wall to punch till his knuckles were bloody. I waited in the living room by the front door until he left without saying goodbye.

People expressed varying degrees of surprise that Dale and I had broken up. "You broke up?!" one friend asked with a look of sympathy. I sensed that she assumed he broke up with me. I explained who broke up with whom but she didn't seem convinced. "Are you alright?" she asked.

"I feel good." I answered. I felt freer than I had in a long time and realized she was incapable of understanding that because she was the kind of person who defined her happiness by the presence of a man in her life.

My aunts had met Dale in the early months of our dating, while I was still on crutches. When I told them I had broken it off with him, they looked grief-stricken and frightened for me. I had felt that look before from people while recovering after the hospital. "I wouldn't let one like him get away." My aunt said. "You can't find too many good ones very easily." She didn't see his out-of-control jealousy and the fact that I had never dated anyone else as an obstacle to my happiness. Or maybe she hadn't considered happiness as an important aspect of any young woman's life. She had been a Catholic nun from the age of fourteen, for thirty years, then quit and quickly got married to a man I would now describe as a latent homosexual.

My mother gave me the same look of grief and fear when she realized Dale and I were definitely off. My mother expressed the sentiment that women should count their blessings as far as having a man in their life, especially a good-looking one who loved me the way Dale did.

As I wandered through the next two years of college, I loved the freedom of doing what I wanted without explanation to anyone. I felt insecure as a lovable partner for any attractive, intelligent young man but I could count many blessings too. I didn't have to work, had my own place to live and a beautiful new car all to myself. Still, I noticed once a month I continued to have a really good cry and didn't really know what I wanted to be when I grew up. In between all of that, I passed most of my classes, despite skipping some and going away for every available weekend to Rebecca's place where I could anonymously party my brains out.

I graduated at the age of 22 with a bachelor's degree in biology. That summer I searched for direction without getting a job, someone knocked on my door.

"Hello, do you have any stains that need to be removed from your carpet or upholstery?" A young man with golden blonde hair and piercing green eyes cheerily asked.

"No." I tried to sound disinterested. I had no idea, of course, that this nineteen-year old would become the father of my two children.

Neutral Buoyancy

One clear, summer morning off the coast of Freeport, Bahamas, with a group of divers, I eagerly put on my gear and jumped into the water. Ten feet below the surface, I had a lot of trouble descending further. I placed my hand at my waist and realized I forgot my weight belt. To go back up and get my weight belt, I would need to signal Sandi, my buddy, then take the chance of having to abort the dive because of my mistake. Since I could see the bottom only 45 feet below me and had no desire to abort the dive, I instead held tight to the boat's anchor line and stubbornly dragged myself down. At 50 feet below surface, I let go of the anchor line and experienced absolute neutral buoyancy for the first time in my life. I marveled at the physical sensation of zero gravity underwater. I attempted to communicate my excitement to the divemaster a few feet away. He appeared distracted by my buoyant breasts rising out of my bathing suit, when I opened my vest to show him I had no weight belt. I soon gave up trying to share my joy and followed the group through giant coral passageways and around endless schools of bright yellow, blue and red fish. I glided effortlessly along like an astronaut in outer space while others squirmed and adjusted their bodies to keep from colliding with marine life and fellow divers.

Neutral buoyancy is achieved underwater when a diver is neither buoyant (rises toward the surface of the water) nor sinking toward the bottom of the sea. When a diver wants her body to rise to the surface, she only need push a button on her vest that transfers air from tank to vest, causing ascent. When a diver wants to descend, she pushes a different button on her vest to expel air trapped inside her vest. The same thing, to a lesser extent, can be achieved with inhalation/exhalation via her lungs. Take in a deep breath underwater and your body ascends a few inches. Empty your lungs and for a moment your body descends a few inches. For two years previous, I struggled with maintaining neutral buoyancy on my dives. It took a mistake for me to understand the delicate balance between taking in and letting go. Also the weight I had been carrying on my weight belt was twice as much as I needed. No amount of air in my vest could have compensated for too much weight on my belt. In my above water life, I also struggled with taking in (accepting) and letting go (forgiveness). Taking in the right amount of air is analogous to accepting events in my life that I couldn't change and had no control over. Letting go of the right amount of air is analogous to forgiving myself and others for any negative thoughts and actions that only held me back from reaching my goals. Learning how to reach a balance between taking in and letting go has helped me in all areas of my life.

"My name is Chase, how are you today?" He stuck out his hand without hesitation.

"Ann." I said with as flat a tone of voice as I could muster while unable to take my eyes off his. I came out from behind my front door and stepped outside, closing it behind me.

"Any stain in your carpet or furniture that I'll bet you I can get out?" He spoke like a natural born salesman.

I decided I would play his game of determination to convince the other. He would try to sell me his "miracle cleaner" and I would persist in "no" till he stopped trying. After about an hour of nonstop talking and demonstrating the miracle cleaner on my car, the concrete driveway, the siding on the house and finally my white tennis shoes, Chase pointed to an old car that circled the block several times.

"It's my work leader telling me I need to move on." He said abruptly.

My little brother Louis, sixteen and no longer little, painted the trim on my house as he watched Chase and me. Chase would convince Louis to give him my phone number. Several hours after Chase left, my phone rang.

"Hi! You remember me? The miracle cleaner guy?" His infectious laugh reached out through the phone.

"Yeah. How did you get my phone number?" I still couldn't believe he was for real.

"Your brother. Are you hungry? I'm fixing to go out to dinner soon and thought I could swing by and pick you up." His enthusiasm was as infectious as his laugh. My game of resistance finally ended. He showed up at my door with a case of miracle cleaner in his arms. "On the house." He announced with a smile and placed it on the front step.

We went to a cheap diner and stayed up all night drinking coffee and talking about our different past, unbelievable present and limitless future.

He embodied fearlessness in every way I imagined a person could. He was gorgeous and he gazed at me as though he thought I was gorgeous.

"Rude, crude and socially unacceptable." He happily declared himself. Chase spoke with boundless enthusiasm for life and dared everyone around him to do the same.

I had done the right thing for most of my life. Doing the wrong thing always proved more fun it seemed. Chase felt like a part of both—bad boy who satisfied my soul's hunger for adventure.

After a day of him working and no sleep, Chase asked me out to dinner again. We went to the same cheap diner and again stayed up till the sun rose from the hot, humid summer horizon. Chase and the group of teenagers he traveled with selling miracle cleaner were driving west toward Kansas City and he promised to keep in touch as he kissed me goodbye. I went to bed that sunny morning and slept till the sun rose again, 22 hours later.

I followed Chase across the state as he moved around with the group selling all-purpose cleaner that only proved profitable for the few older ones in charge. I had just graduated college a couple of months earlier. I paid my dues as far as hard work. It felt like time for crazy fun and Chase became the vehicle for me to release pent-up wanderlust and just plain lust for that matter.

Three months later, I drove my brand new Datsun 280ZX 900 miles to visit Chase in Pennsylvania, where he lived with his father, stepmother and half-siblings. It was heaven driving that sweet little sports car across the country in October, when the weather was perfect and the fall colors were just beginning to show themselves.

When I arrived, heaven turned into hell as I spent time with his family. His long-suffering stepmother had stuck by his father through years of physical violence and alcoholism. One night while I was there, Chase's father woke everyone up at 2:00 in the morning, speaking with more certain yet slurred words than he ever used sober. He pointed then poked me with his index finger the way my father would when he was angry. It occurred to me that Chase's father was actually terrified, by his many past mistakes and uncertain future. I didn't imagine I would ever, as an independent adult, be part of any violence like I had seen in Chase's family and like I had grown up with in my own family.

Six months later, I followed Chase to his aunt and uncle's boat dock on a lake in Tennessee. I couldn't identify the uneasiness I felt and assumed I was in the throes of wild love. Young and determined, no one could tell me what to do with my life.

During my time away from Chase I continued to go bar hopping with Rebecca. One night in a loud, crowded, smoke-filled bar I knew I was ready to quit spending my evenings like this and start raising a family. It's not that I desired being in a long-term relationship with any man. I had simply crossed over into certainty about motherhood.

A year and a half after meeting him, I asked Chase to come live with me in the house I bought with the settlement money from the lawsuit against the electric company. For most of that winter and spring we played house. Life was easy. Every day I went to my job at a hospital blood lab and Chase found work as a temporary painter, car mechanic, construction worker or whatever else became available.

Within five months, the doctor told me I was pregnant. Raising a baby without its father did not seem possible to me so I began considering getting married to Chase. "How do you know when it's the right one?" I asked my friends at the hospital laboratory where I worked. I asked anyone I could find how he or she knew when it was the right time to get married. Everyone seemed to have vague answers with words like "love" used in so many ways, I felt more confused.

When the pregnancy test came up positive, Chase was ecstatic. I was excited but worried about how I would explain it to my parents. I felt embarrassed that I had not planned something important as pregnancy.

"Ann's pregnant!" Chase burst out in the middle of my parents' living room.

"Oh…well…congratulations." My father spoke. My mother looked at me with that familiar pity I knew from the hospital.

With a baby on the way I felt an urgency to start choosing the right thing to do. I didn't want my baby to come into the world without a father, so I married Chase in the Catholic Church I grew up in, on a beautiful Wednesday evening in

September. I loved planning the dresses for the five bridesmaids and the tuxedos for the groomsmen. I loved the fresh gardenia corsages for the mothers and grandmothers and the mixture of them with lilies and white roses in my bouquet. At four months pregnant, it felt like fate that the first gown I tried on at the bridal shop fit me perfectly and I got it at half the ordered price. Its original client had left it before the last payment came due. I even liked the priest who performed the wedding ceremony.

Chase and I went to Nassau, Bahamas for our honeymoon. We gambled at a casino on Paradise Island. Chase tipped the change girl, who told us which dollar slot machines to go to next for a winning pull. We profited $700.00 in one evening. We made friends with some other couples at the hotel where we stayed. Chase was always ready to go out and have a good time and I liked the ease he seemed to have in social situations. On the plane flying back home, Chase made friends with a man who claimed to have some great cocaine and invited us to the back to try some. I was grateful to have the excuse that I couldn't do any drugs or alcohol because I was pregnant. I ignored the uneasiness I felt listening to this stranger give us his address and phone number and offer to sell us some premium snow, after Chase had gone to the back and tried some.

Chase was all of 21 when we got married and I naively assumed he was ready for what was to come since he agreed to get married.

One night, a few months after the wedding, we went to my parents' house for dinner and played some cards at the dinner table. My father always kidded around about communicating with hand gestures about what was in his hand. Everyone but Chase knew the joke. As Chase and I climbed out of the car later, at home, he suddenly expressed his feeling of a conspiracy against him during the card game, then pushed me down in the snow. My eight months pregnant body fell hard as my heart raced. I walked toward the next door neighbor's house and threatened to wake them up if he didn't calm down. His excuse for being angry was he was tired and that my dad was cheating at cards. We walked into the house, Chase to the bedroom and me to the kitchen. Something told me he was not calmed down. I was very pregnant and in no condition to fight and saw no other alternative but to call the police. As I spoke to the operator, I heard my voice struggle to catch my breath. Suddenly, Chase's hand reached from behind me and hung up the phone.

"What do you think you're doing?" he scolded. I said nothing and he walked back to the bedroom. I paced the living room, wondering what to do next when I heard a sturdy knock on the front door. I opened it and three uniformed policemen stood there. I started sobbing with relief as they asked me about where Chase was and did we have any firearms in the house. I told them he did have a rifle in the bedroom and pointed in that direction. They pulled out their guns and aimed them down the hall while I wondered if all this precaution was necessary. Chase was lying in bed, under the covers, claiming to have the rifle at his side when they questioned him. When he quickly realized they weren't going to back down, after they told him to come out from under the covers, he agreed to stop being a threat to his wife. The officers assured me that he seemed okay and did not have his rifle with him in bed. I must have calmed down enough to go to bed that night but what kind of denial was I practicing for the next year that we lived together? Was I unconsciously behaving like my mother had for years, pretending it wasn't that bad? Or staying so busy with the chores of motherhood I really didn't stop to notice.

Two weeks before my twenty fifth birthday, Will was born. When I held him for the first time his big blue eyes stared into mine with a recognition. I thought, "My God, this little human being just came out of my body! What do I do now?"

I fell in love with that incredible little miracle that was my son. I spent hours just staring at him. I watched with amazement that this tiny body knew how to yawn, sneeze, and suckle at my breast. I studied biology in college with a fascination for how my body had healed after injury. I studied my son with a fascination for how human beings grow and develop. Every day, sometimes every hour, a new discovery for both of us emerged. His ten little toes were especially fascinating given I had few left on my foot.

I learned that really raising a child was an exhausting and love-filled job. With a colicky baby like Will, it became a lesson in patience too. He cried so much I couldn't trust anyone who didn't already love him to have the stamina and patience to care for him. I was lucky to be able to afford to stay home from work to be with my baby. After six months maternity leave from my job as a medical technologist (lab technician in a lab that tested various body fluids, but mostly blood), I felt compelled to stay home and raise Will full time.

Then one night a friend confessed to me that Chase had screwed some woman two months after our wedding. No surprise to some of my friends, but for me, immersed in motherhood and buried under denial, I didn't see it coming. An old strategy I had used it childhood and in the Burn Unit, stoicism in the midst of pain, became my choice for dealing with my emotional shock. The sad part was Chase didn't seem to notice my feelings had changed toward him.

I decided I wanted at least one more child and knew deep inside that this marriage would not last and let myself become pregnant a second time.

One day I brought Will to the pediatrician because of a growing lump on the side of his chest. "Isn't ten months too young for a baby to get cancer?" I asked. The pediatrician said no and sent us to an oncologist at the children's hospital. I carried Will past many children with bald heads in the arms of worried parents. The doctor examined Will's lump with an excited curiosity. I noticed and suppressed my urge to hit or yell at the man. The doctor said let's cut out the lump with a simple fast surgery and biopsy it. A few days later I handed over Will to two hospital attendants who wheeled him down a hall in a pediatric gurney as he looked at me and screamed for help. Why didn't they just knock him out before he left? My guilt weighed me down and Chase and I waited for an hour till a nurse brought Will to us crying once again. Chase grabbed him from the nurse and tried to comfort him. I pulled off the scratchy sweater I had on and anxiously begged to hold Will. He finally did stop crying as he settled into my arms. Later the results showed no cancer, just a swollen gland in an unusual place on the body. I understood a little better what my parents must have gone through years earlier with my brother Kenny.

By Christmas, six weeks before Will's first birthday, Chase had been arrested twice for driving while intoxicated, wrecked my car with over $4000.00 worth of damages, lost three jobs, and had sex with other women God only knows how many times. I told no one, especially Chase, that I was pregnant.

Just after New Year's Day, one month before Will's first birthday, I asked Chase to leave my house. I say my house because it was. I had paid all the bills, even bought my own wedding ring because Chase never had any money because he never kept his job. What the hell had I done getting hooked up with someone like him? I mistook lust for love and I thought a child should be with his father. Sadly, it took the extensive damage to my car to push me over the edge. Maybe it was the last straw or maybe I valued my car more than myself.

Chase went to Texas I heard. He still didn't know I was pregnant with our second child. It seemed to me that if I told him I was pregnant, he might not leave and I'd be stuck with him even longer.

When I was four and a half months pregnant, Chase knocked on the door one afternoon and climbed into bed with me. I felt dangerously drawn to him.

When a person grows up in an environment of tyranny where individual decisions were immediately squashed and contradictions loomed everywhere, she begins to step outside of reason for her choices. Chase was a big step outside of reason. He represented everything my upbringing told me I should avoid and that intrigued me. Unconsciously, I used Chase as retribution against a childhood filled with betrayal. He became forbidden fruit that even my parents were forced to swallow, until I realized my marriage to him was dangerous to me and my children.

When I was six months pregnant, Chase knocked on the front door with his girlfriend in tow, demanding I lend him my camera purchased long before I met him. I threw a pint of eggshell latex paint on him and ran out of the front door to tell our across the street neighbor to "Call 911!" The police officer who arrived soon after and my parents all looked at me as if I had lost my mind. My mother expressed more concern about what the neighbors would think than about Chase intruding. I, on the other hand, felt liberated in expressing the rage building in me.

The day of our divorce finally arrived! With a six month old daughter and a two year old son to take care of, I felt giddy with the relief of leaving the life I lived with Chase behind me. I soon realized being married to Chase was like having another child—a child who never grew and always demanded more.

Chase would soon become the same kind of father that he had—absent. I counted on him not being around, even convinced myself I didn't need a man to be a father to my kids. I had my brother and my father to serve as uncle and grandfather to Will and Annie.

It was easy to not look at myself and instead blame Chase as responsible party in this mess of a relationship that mercifully ended with divorce. It wasn't a failure since two beautiful children came out of it and many times in my life the presence of

Will and Annie has kept my focus on doing the best for them, thus saving me from bad choices that could have been legally or physically dangerous. I wanted to hurt Chase the way I felt he had hurt me but I always stopped with the thought what would happen after I slashed his tires on the truck I financed? What would happen if I paid someone to beat the crap out of him? I could go to jail was the answer which meant I would lose my children. The thought of losing Will and Annie kept me from acting on my rage. My sweet, precious babies saved me in so many ways, particularly from taking revenge on their father.

My rage came out in my sleep one night. I was a wild dog with big teeth, in a small, empty white room with Chase opposite me, naked, at my level, on his hands and knees. I unleashed my ferocity by biting off his penis. Blood sprayed everywhere, hiding his severed member and I felt relief. Chase cowered in the corner, whimpering in his pain. The dream alone purged my immense anger at Chase and I could go forward in my life without endangering Will, Annie, Chase or myself.

On the day of our divorce, when Annie was almost seven months old, I had gotten everything I thought I needed and wanted. Two beautiful, healthy children and freedom from any man telling me what to do. Had I somehow felt more lovable being partnered with a good-looking man? Had we both been attracted to the other because of the sense that intimacy was not a requirement? I told myself Chase was the origin and his disappearance the solution to all my problems. He was an easy scapegoat. Although I was not clear about what I wanted in a relationship with a man, I was very clear about what I didn't want. Chase personified what I didn't want in a man. I didn't want a husband/boyfriend/lover who was a father to me, telling me what to do, asking where I was going or what I was doing. I had escaped the intrusiveness of my father and a possessive boyfriend and now the craziness of a relationship with a husband that felt more like a third child than a partner.

Walking away from Chase left me looking virtuous. My friends like Rebecca breathed a sigh of relief after he was gone. I have read that statistically, women don't benefit from divorce as much as men do. Often women change residence and socioeconomic class for the worse, while men maintain and even improve materially. Because of more money at my disposal, my post-divorce lifestyle resembled that of a man's more than a woman's. Because of the material comforts in our lives and the good health of both myself and my children, I easily pushed away the memory of what became a nightmare with Chase. I jokingly told friends and myself that unless I met Jesus Christ reincarnated, I would not get married again. I even convinced myself I was too busy with kids and life to date any man.

I relied more on my parents and siblings, most who lived within the same city. My youngest sister Tina, in fact, lived with me, Will and Annie.

To keep some semblance of peace in my Catholic family, I had Will and Annie baptized in the same church where I married Chase. I had filed for divorce months before but the priest didn't seem to be concerned about that. As children we were told divorced people were excommunicated unless an annulment was approved. Excommunication sounded like a bargain compared to marriage to Chase. I avoided the Catholic church altogether after that anyway.

Truth was I felt terrified to get close to/depend on any man. Chase with his selfish, immature impulsive behavior gave me an escape from having to look at myself in the mirror of relationship. I thought Dale and I had a great one until the green-eyed monster barged in. Why was it great? Because he really loved me, scars and all. Hadn't Chase been that way too? Then what was it? What was keeping me from having a great relationship without the invading monsters? Me.

I looked around and saw only dysfunctional relationships. Relationships that required a greater fear of being alone than being confined with a person who could change into something I wouldn't recognize.

When I announced my plans to file for divorce, my parents sat me down and explained that infidelity was one of those things that a person worked through in marriage. I turned to my father, who seemed to be the boss of my mother's identity and said "Would your advice be the same if you were talking to Joey?" (my brother who had recently married)

"Well, no." he answered with a bewildered look. I didn't have to say anything more and neither did he. I had heard my mother and other women discuss the virtue of commitment as if the more they suffered, the greater the accomplishment. I could not understand that way of thinking. If that was marriage, I preferred to be unmarried for the rest of my life. Was the whole world being conned with the idea that suffering was virtuous unto itself? Yes, of course I already knew that. At the same time, however, having scars (physical proof of suffering) was shameful. These contradictions screamed of the craziness in a world I wanted to escape from but couldn't. I realized no one could tell me what to think, I had to decide for myself—both a grueling and freeing discovery.

I didn't want to be close, didn't want to expect a guy to be faithful sexually cause wasn't that like asking my body to grow a new leg? Doesn't a man eventually get tired of doing the right thing? Doesn't a man really want a woman who's beautiful on the outside and if she's not she needs to tolerate his imperfections?

I went to a counselor a few times and her advice to me was "You have good instincts, trust them!" Okay, my instincts told me to depend on myself, love my children before they grow up too quickly and enjoy everything I can about life.

Getting pregnant, being pregnant and delivering a healthy boy, then eighteen months later a healthy girl, was easy for my young, strong body. I had many reasons to be grateful.

Having enough money to support my kids and I was also a reason for gratitude and the continuation of my fierce independence.

After the divorce, I bought a house a mile down the street on a cul-de-sac. It became a haven for Will, Annie and I. Less car traffic and more socializing with families our same age. The only thing we lacked was a father which I stubbornly compensated for by telling myself it didn't matter.

Will reminded me that it did by asking "Where's my daddy?" after he started going to school. Annie didn't ask. I told myself that even the married women with children I saw in the neighborhood lived a solitary life like mine since their husbands were often gone at work. I had the added bonus of a large number of siblings who lived nearby and were wonderful uncles, aunts and their children cousins to Will and Annie.

The only mother Will and Annie ever knew was a mother with lots of scars all over her body and a left leg ten inches shorter than her right leg. I wanted them both to be comfortable with my unusual body so I made a daily game of my short leg. When they were toddlers, I sat on the floor to play at their level. Often I took off my prosthesis because it was easier and more comfortable to simply crawl around on my hands and knees. One day I lifted my short leg in the air, bent it at the knee and barked like a puppy while I moved it the way a dog's head does. Will and Annie played along immediately as only children so beautifully do. They petted, hugged and talked to the "doggie". Soon they referred to my short leg as "Mama's ruff", since the sound of the barking I made was "ruff,ruff". One day Annie saw a cartoon with a peg leg character and excitedly told me "Look, Mama, he's got a ruff too!" I still laugh remembering that. Never again would I use the word stump in reference to my body.

Enjoying my life included joining the local chain health spa. Will and Annie came along before they reached school age and stayed with the in-house sitter. I bribed them on days they asked to stay home with ice cream after my workouts. It felt great to get back into shape and move like a dancer in aerobics classes and enjoy a massage after that.

The first Thanksgiving at our new house, my siblings, their partners, children and my parents came over for a big dinner. Everyone laughed, ate and talked long after dark. As I talked to my sister Marie she said "Bill and I are going to Cancun for a week in January. Wanna go with us?"

"I'll stay with the kids." My brother Louis offered.

How could I refuse?

I didn't.

Like a waking dream, I found myself flying on a plane to Mexico, with my children back home in the loving arms of their uncle, with whom they were thrilled to spend time.

From white January cold in Missouri to Mexican blue sky and waters in Cancun, I had to catch my breath. Your children are fine, you're going to be okay and you're going to enjoy yourself, my better sense told me.

We signed up for a one day snorkeling trip to Cozumel. Twenty adults crammed onto a twenty foot boat then set free with snorkels and fins after a short ride. My world expanded that day I looked under the water and noticed scuba divers at the bottom looking like they were having way more fun than I was.

"I want to try scuba diving with you guys tomorrow." I told my sister and her husband that night as we finished our margaritas and homemade corn chips and salsa.

The next morning we found the dive hut at the shore of the deserted beach where our lovely little bungalows rested.

"Hello, my name is Fernando. How can I help you?" The friendly young Mexican man with bleached blonde hair and

Caribbean blue eyes said as he shook hands with each of us.

"I want to try scuba diving. Can you do that for me?" I asked gently.

I felt the sky and sea burst open above and below me and something told me then his answer would be yes.

See 1st World Books at:

www.1stWorldPublishing.com

See our classic collection at:

www.1stWorldLibrary.com

www.ingramcontent.com/pod-product-compliance
Lightning Source LLC
Chambersburg PA
CBHW021107090426
42738CB00006B/534